IMAGES OF WAR

THE GERMAN ARMY ON THE WESTERN FRONT 1917-1918

RARE PHOTOGRAPHS FROM WARTIME ARCHIVES

DAVID BILTON

Pen & Sword
MILITARY

First published in Great Britain in 2007 by
PEN & SWORD MILITARY
an imprint of
Pen & Sword Books Ltd,
47 Church Street, Barnsley,
South Yorkshire.
S70 2AS

Copyright © David Bilton, 2007

ISBN 978-1-84415-502-6

The right of David Bilton to be identified as Author of this Work
has been asserted by him in accordance with the
Copyright, Designs and Patents Act 1988.

A CIP catalogue record for this book is available
from the British Library

Printed and bound in Great Britain by CPI UK

Pen & Sword Books Ltd incorporates the imprints of
Pen & Sword Aviation, Pen & Sword Maritime,
Pen & Sword Military, Pen & Sword Select, Pen & Sword Military Classics,
Leo Cooper, Wharncliffe Local History

For a complete list of Pen & Sword titles please contact:
PEN & SWORD BOOKS LIMITED
47 Church Street, Barnsley, South Yorkshire, S70 2AS, England.
E-mail: enquiries@pen-and-sword.co.uk
Website: www.pen-and-sword.co.uk

Contents

Acknowledgements

Once again a big and meaningful thank you to my family who were all pleased that it was supposed to be more of a picture book than my previous efforts. What would I do without Anne Coulson to read my proofs or the Prince Consort's Library to assist me in my research? Thank you. As always it was a pleasure to work with the wonderful team at Pen & Sword.

Any errors of omission or commission are mine alone.

Even with shortages, life could be convivial behind the lines.

Introduction

At the start of 1917, Germany was fighting on both the Western and Eastern Fronts as well as contributing substantial numbers of troops to the fighting on the Southern Front, the Balkans and in the Middle East; tens of thousands of men were also involved in Home Defence and occupation duties in the captured territories.

On the Western Front alone, the German lines stretched for over four hundred miles, starting in the north on the Belgian coast, passing through the wet plains of Flanders down into the chalk flatlands of the Somme, continuing through the hills of Champagne and ending in the mountainous area leading to the Swiss border on the eastern flank. Facing them were the armies of Belgium, France and her colonies, Britain and the British Empire, with a division of Russian troops; these were to be joined during the year by troops from Portugal and the United States, although the German High Command deduced that the latter would not be effective until the spring of 1918.

As well as the military problems on the different war fronts that needed solutions there was a further non-military front to take into account - the Home Front; here there were problems of a different kind. There were food and coal shortages that affected productivity and health (especially among the young, whose physical development was adversely affected, and the old, who suffered increased mortality rates). Manpower was short; the armed forces had first call on any production, and essentials like soap had become scarce; ersatz products, like coffee made from acorns and chicory, became the norm for those who could not afford the prices of the Black Market or were unable to get into the countryside at the weekend to buy food directly from the farmers – weekend excursions that became known to the population as the 'Hamsterfahrt' (Hamster journey). The cereal and potato harvests had dropped by over fifty percent by early 1916 and bread (K-brot - war bread) was made from oat and rice meal, ground beans, peas and corn meal. Butter was available only to the rich; its replacement was made from curdled milk, sugar and food colouring. Similarly, cooking oil was replaced by extracts from red beet, carrots, turnips and spices, fats by a mixture of crushed cockchafers (beetles) and linden wood. Neither was sausage, a staple food, safe from economy measures: it was now produced from animal scraps, plant fibres and water.

Clothing was likewise in short supply and, when available, was supplemented by material such as paper – technically this was known as stretching supplies, and indeed when it got wet it actually stretched! Mounting casualties, with no sign of victory, had a negative effect upon people's attitudes, commitment to the war and productivity. The use of schools for military purposes, coupled with a shortage of school teachers, meant that many children received little education; an upside to this was that they were available to help in factories and on farms, but many of them turned to crime and the crime rate increased – this was blamed on the lack of male role models available to keep them in check. On top of this, the winter of 1916/1917 was the coldest for years with the temperature dropping to -30°C, forcing the closure of restaurants, stores and theatres, due to an acute shortage of coal that industry had first call on. The 'Turnip Winter', where children stole each other's rations and women worried more about their children's hunger than about their husbands at the front, was not an auspicious start to 1917.

Increasing instability, demands for manpower in industry on the Home Front, and extended commitment at the front meant that the German army in manpower terms was overstretched even to hold the line defensively, let alone mount an offensive in the west on what was considered the decisive front. A further drain on German manpower had been the German and Allied offensives in France; during the fighting of 1916 on the Somme and at Verdun, Germany had incurred enormous casualties. Estimated losses on the Western Front alone amounted to over 960,000, with materiel losses of nearly 2000 field guns, over 250 mortars and 1000 machine guns. German peace proposals at the end of 1916 were rejected so the war would continue.

In 1917 the uneasy state of Germany offered some encouragement to the Allied camp; a reduced bread ration in April had caused disturbances and riots and, in July, there were mutinies on several battleships. Hindenburg and Ludendorff threatened to resign unless the Chancellor retired, which he duly did on 13 July, and, most disappointingly to the Army High Command, the Reichstag passed a resolution demanding a peace of understanding.

As a result of the previous year's fighting, the German army of 1917 was severely stretched, and during 1917 the general reserve stood between four and six divisions; positional change was needed and would soon come. By 1918 further events had transformed the Western Front and the stalemate no longer existed – mobile warfare had returned and eventually the war would be decided one way or another.

It is not the purpose of this book to analyse in detail the strategic, tactical, political or economic reasons for this situation or its results, but merely to chronicle the events of 1917 and 1918 in words (briefly) and pictures – almost all from the German side of the wire and mostly concentrated on their British opponents. I have not tried to chronicle every battle in detail but have used the Battle for Arras to show the typical experiences of a front line unit and soldier. Neither is it a chronological photographic record; it is an attempt to provide a snapshot of the experiences of the German Army on the Western Front over a two-year period. Similarly the day-to-day chronology is taken from the German point of view. Not every day is listed; for any day apparently missing read 'Im Westen nichts Neues' – 'In the West nothing new', or, as it is usually translated, 'All quiet on the Western Front'.

Chapter One

1917

The situation at the end of 1916

'As far as human judgement could foresee everything pointed to the Western Front as the scene of our chief defensive fighting in 1917', wrote Ludendorff in his memoirs. The preceding months had involved the final stages of the battle of the Somme and the French victories at Verdun, and, as a result, OHL (*Oberst Heeresleitung* – German High Command) issued instructions on the role of the Siegfried Stellung (Hindenburg Line): 'Just as in times of peace, we build fortresses, so we are now building rearward defences. Just as we have kept clear of our fortresses, so shall we keep at a distance from these rearward defences.' A few days later, as a result of the high casualty rate caused by the pattern of defence on the Somme, OHL stipulated that in future defence was to be in depth but elastic. 'Out went deep dug-outs and continuous trench lines, to be replaced by concrete bunkers, surrounded by obstacle belts and sited for mutual support. Gone was the rigid holding of the forward trenches packed with infantrymen. In came flexibility, defence in depth, a huge increase in infantry fire power, streamlined command and control and numerous tactical innovations.'

At the end of 1916 the Hindenburg line was to be regarded as a 'factor of safety' and there was no intention of voluntarily retiring to it; however, by the middle of January, General von Kuhl summed up the situation at the principal General Staff officers' conference: 'We can no longer reckon on the old troops; there is no doubt but that in the past summer and autumn our troops have been fearfully harried and wasted'. British Fifth Army winter operations made the situation even worse and by the end of January it was acknowledged that the positions presently held by the German Army 'were bad, the troops worn out' and that they were probably not in a condition to stand such defensive battles as 'The Hell of the Somme' again, (the 94 German divisions that had fought on the Somme were classed by the British *Official History of the Great War* as being in a 'dire state'). After the war the German *Official History* acknowledged the losses of killed and wounded during 1916 as 1,400,000, of whom 800,000 were between July and October. One writer summed up the intensity and sacrifice of the battle after the war: 'Whenever you see a fighter who was there at the Somme, bow low to the ground, because you simply do not know what he did for you.' Even with this level of loss and commitment, Ludendorff was not prepared to retire, although 'withdrawal was eminently sensible for a belligerent on the strategic defensive.'

The weather conditions at the end of the year were appalling. Heavy rain and snowfalls, resulting in severe mud, encumbered movement and made life a misery; mud over a metre deep was common; later the conditions were acknowledged to be worse than a year later on the Ypres front. Conditions on both sides of No Man's Land were equally bad: rifles, caked with mud, were in many cases unusable; men sank into the mud and had to be pulled out; with no shelter from the rain, it was almost impossible to maintain health and fitness; illness was rampant among the German troops but there was little that could be done to alleviate the problem of colds, chills, gastro-intestinal illnesses, lung disease, rheumatism and kidney infections. There was no way to ever get dry; it was so wet that one German soldier wrote home that the leather and clothing on the troops were actually rotting while in use. The British *Official History* also makes comment on the conditions: 'the state of the ground of the Somme battlefield during December was such as was probably never surpassed on the Western Front.' It was a wilderness of mud and waterlogged trenches that were accessible only at night. The mud 'took on an aggressive, wolf-like guise, and like a wolf could pull down and swallow the lonely wanderer in the darkness.'

By 1917 a well stocked canteen like this was a thing of the past.

How the war had started out – an adventure to be celebrated with flowers – by 1917 there were no such celebrations to send the men off to the war.

However, the bad weather had one benefit: there was little firing and as a result it was possible for troops of both sides to move around freely at times without being shot at; friend and foe could climb out of their holes in broad daylight to stretch their fatigued bodies. But when the weather changed, the artillery would start the war again.

On 17 December, Crown Prince Rupprecht, in a secret order, congratulated the troops of the *First* and *Second* Armies for their courage during the battle of the Somme: 'the enemy sought to break through and attacked repeatedly; each attempt failed, the only gain being a narrow strip of utterly ruined terrain'. To the German Army it was a victory: 'The greatest battle of the war, perhaps the greatest of all time has been won', he wrote to his troops. Although it might have been classed as a victory, General von Kuhl regarded the casualty rate as detrimental to the functioning of the army: 'the casualties suffered by Germany hit it harder than did those of the Allies' and each year it was more difficult to replace the losses. The position of the German Army at the end of 1916 was ably summed up by the commander of 27 *Infantry Division*: 'The formations which were deployed during the Battle of the Somme were very worn down physically and their nerves were badly affected. The huge gaps torn in the ranks could only be filled out by returning wounded, nineteen-year-olds who were too young, or by combing out from civilian occupations, men who, to a large extent, due to their physical condition or mental attitude, could not be regarded as fully effective troops'.

Withdrawal to the Siegfried Stellung

No matter how bad the conditions nor how worn out the troops, the war continued. The 1917 season started on 1 January, with the capture of a British position – Hope Post near Beaumont Hamel. However, the occupancy was short and on 5 January it was lost along with a neighbouring post and fifty-six prisoners. Further losses occurred on the night of 10 January near Beaumont Hamel in men and trenches, while the intended counterattack was broken up by British artillery fire. On 11 January, Munich Trench fell to a British attack, but the assault by 11 British Division was checked and the positions near Muck Trench held. The rest of the month was relatively quiet and the frost made life easier in many ways. Further minor British attacks in early February captured a number of useful observation points that stopped the Germans from observing future preparations.

With the certainty of further British attacks, the army was to be ordered back to the Siegfried Stellung. This defensive line, with a depth of between six and eight thousand yards, ran east from Laffaux to Cerny-en-Laonnais on the Chemin des Dames ridge where it joined the front-line defences. Considerable effort had been put into these fortifications, using mass production techniques: 'all the woodwork was uniform in design, the dug-out doors, for example, being turned out to a pattern from the sawmills…by the thousands. There were comparatively shallow dug-outs of ferro-concrete…to a fixed pattern and…also mined dug-outs.' Three belts of barbed wire protected the trenches, each ten to fifteen yards deep, with a five-yard gap between each. The fortifications were constructed initially by Russian POWs and later by troops, Belgian civilian conscripts and skilled German craftsmen - eventually around 65,000 men were employed on this task on a daily basis.

The retirement to the new positions was code-named 'Alberich' (a malicious dwarf from the Niebelung Saga) and the Army Group was directed to draw up detailed plans for its execution. Plans were also made to turn the zone between the new positions and the front line into a desert. 'Not only were all military buildings to be dismantled, depots to be withdrawn, railways to be torn up, craters to be blown in the roads; but so as far as possible, every town and village, every building in them, was to be destroyed by fire or explosive; every tree, even fruit trees, was to be cut down, or "ringed" to ensure that it died; civilians were to be removed; and wells filled up or polluted, though not poisoned.' It was decided to leave between ten and fifteen thousand civilians – almost all were children, their mothers, and the aged – along with thousands of weapons, items of equipment and buildings carefully booby-trapped to kill or maim the advancing Allied soldiers. The civilians were to be left in Nesle, Ham, Noyon and a few smaller places in the intact houses for the advancing troops to look after; the remainder were taken away to work in the fields and factories. This programme was scheduled to start on 9 February and end on 15 March. Only then could the troops begin their retirement; by 20 March all troops should be in their new positions.

As often with the best-laid plans, all did not go as planned; British attacks met with stiff resistance, but although prisoners clearly indicated that a retirement would take place in the near future, the severity of the fighting indicated that it would be later rather than sooner on the British Fourth Army front. Conditions were so bad that men who were trapped in the mud died of exposure before they could be dug out. The first withdrawal on the British Fourth Army front took place during the morning of 14 March in secrecy, and it was not until fires were seen burning in St Pierre-Vaast Wood that a forward observing artillery officer crossed No Man's Land. Over the next two days, the troops withdrew from trench to trench, using sniper fire and machine guns to halt any pursuit. However, by 16 March, the first full marching day, the main body of the troops were retiring to the Siegfried Stellung and by 18 March four armies were withdrawing on a front of 110 miles followed by six enemy armies. By the end of March, the complete Alberich timetable was in British hands and they were now aware that the original withdrawals were not part of the plan. The whole defence line was not complete; indeed, this was the reason for the need to hold on to certain outpost villages. However, by 5 April, the retirement was complete reducing the amount of line to be defended and increasing the number of men available to counter any future enemy attacks; supply was also easier. However, it was purely a defensive move.

While the High Command advocated defence, the Entente was gearing up for the offence. Both sides were developing tactics designed to make each other's lives more unpleasant. Fluid defence in depth, rapid deployment of local reserves and not every attack being countered, was countered by the British with the 'box' and 'creeping' barrage with little or no preparation and the night assault. The next battles were to be against the British at Arras and the French on the Chemin des Dames.

The battles for Arras and the Chemin des Dames and the French Mutiny
The Battle of Arras, most famous for the Canadian success at Vimy Ridge, started on 9 April, and continued well into May, with further subsidiary attacks in June. Originally organised as a prior subsidiary to the Nivelle Offensive, it became the major Allied attack when the French offensive failed and was extended past its original design to cover-up the French mutinies. Although it was a success in both effect on the German troops and the territory recovered, it is still overshadowed by the Somme and Passchendaele, even though the daily casualty rate was higher than either.

Facing the British were strong defences, especially south of the Neuville St. Vaast to Bailleul road; after the first system of trenches, were three or four further lines from seventy-five to one hundred and fifty yards apart, linked by communication trenches at least every hundred yards; behind that was a support line and the formidable Siegfried Stellung. South of the River Scarpe was a very strong, heavily wired reserve line, about three miles from the front – the Wancourt-Feuchy line, while on the northern side it curved back up to five miles. From the river at Athies to Farbus was the intermediate Point du Jour line that ran along the steep eastern slope of Vimy Ridge; behind that was a newly constructed reserve line, the Drocourt-Quéant switch. Holding these positions were troops of above average quality: *11, 17, 18, 23, 24, 79 Divisions* and *220 Reserve Division* together with *14 Bavarian* and *1 Bavarian Reserve Divisions*.

During February, identifications from raids had shown that the Canadian Corps was closing in and concentrating on the Vimy plateau, and the increased activity in the British positions was noted, particularly the work carried out on railways and roads, the increase in transport and the arrival of artillery units. From 19 March, countermeasures were undertaken: reinforcements were brought up in the form of fresh divisions, more heavy artillery, aircraft and machine gun units with six divisions going to *Sixth Army* as a mobile reserve. Behind the lines at Douai, 'mountains of shells' were stored and further work was carried out on the defences. However, much of the work was nullified by increase in enemy artillery fire and there were problems with the existing defences from a defender's point of view. 'The new divisions which were put into the line complained that their predecessors had neglected the trenches and wire; now the bombardment, combined with the bad weather, made adequate repair almost impossible. The strain upon the troops was severe in the extreme', and even though the enemy artillery barrage had not properly started many of the new and existing batteries were put out of action.

On the morning 4 April, the British gas barrage temporarily silenced the greater portion of the artillery. Two of the defending divisions were the chief recipients of the gas: while *11 Division* suffered few casualties, the casualty rate in *14 Bavarian Division* was much greater. This had a demoralising effect on their future combat performance, so much so that they surrendered more readily when the enemy attacked on 9 April. The enemy bombardment caused severe damage and problems. 'The forward trenches became lines of shell-holes, and those in the rear suffered only a little less seriously – the wire, bad to begin with, disappeared altogether in many places, and fresh stocks to repair it could not be brought forward… section by section, as the defences were systematically reduced'. It was not only wire that could not be brought up: 'it took six hours to bring up rations from the regimental headquarters to the front line, a distance of about a mile in most cases, and towards the end of the bombardment none could be moved in certain sections'. Whole units disappeared from view and control: 'from the 6th to the 8th, the *51st Regiment* had no news at all from one of its companies in the first line. On the latter morning a patrol got through to it, to return with a report that the defences were destroyed, that the men had been without sleep and almost without food since the beginning of the bombardment, and that losses were heavy…the *10th Grenadier Regiment* in the same

Life on the Home Front – an absence of men.

division… had 181 casualties during the bombardment'. Troops using the deep dug-outs were safe from the shellfire, but the entrances were not and many were blown in. Enemy counter battery fire was so effective that one division reported that it did not have a single battery able to perform at full capacity. And neither the previously mentioned 'mountains of ammunition' nor the extra heavy artillery arrived at the front, so that when the enemy attacked there was a general shortage of ammunition with which to delay the attacking forces.

The British history, *Military Operations France and Belgium 1917*, describes what happened from the German perspective using their own regimental histories: 'on the right of the British attack on the 9th April stood the German *18th Reserve Division*. It faced the left brigade of the (British) 21st Division - the only brigade of that division which took part in the original attack – the 30th Division and the right brigade of the 56th Division. This was the most fortunate of the German divisions. Its main defences were the two trenches of the strong Hindenburg or Siegfried system, though its third trench, the *Artillerieschutsistellung*, was shallow and without shelters. All three regiments were in line, each having two battalions in the three trenches mentioned, and the third in reserve. On the German left the *84th Reserve Regiment* lost a portion of the Hindenburg Line on the afternoon of the 9th April, but recovered it by a counterattack next evening. The *86th Reserve Regiment*, in the centre, repulsed the attack of the 30th Division. It was only the *31st Reserve Regiment*, on the right, which suffered seriously in the attack of the 9th. Its right turned by the fall of Neuville Vitasse, it formed a flank facing north in a communication trench south of and parallel to the Neuville-Wancourt road. On 10 April it was ordered to withdraw to a new line running about a thousand yards north-west of Wancourt and Guémappe; but the troops in the salient immediately south of Neuville were nearly all mopped up by the bombers of the 56th Division. Early on the 10th, a battalion of the *121st Reserve Regiment* was placed at the disposal of the *38th Reserve Division*. This battalion belonged to the *26th Reserve Division*, which had just been relieved at Bullecourt. All the remainder of the division had gone back to rest areas, but this unit happened to be still on the platform at Cagnicourt awaiting a train, and was marched north into the battle. Later in the day two battalions of the *26th Division*, one of the so-called "counterattack divisions", were added as a reserve.'

'The *18th Reserve Division* was driven back but never really broken, as were those further north. It was left in action until the 14th April, and its casualties were not very high: according to its own account, 62 officers and 1,702 other ranks.' But not all divisions were as lucky as *18 Reserve Division*. With its left flank resting on the Neuville to Wancourt road, *17 Division* held the line from Neuville Vitasse to Tilloy lez Mofflaines, a sector about to be attacked by the British 3, 14 and 56 Divisions. Casualties would be high.

'The *163rd Regiment*, on the left, had three companies annihilated at Neuville Vitasse. On the evening of the 9th April it repulsed the British attack against the Wancourt-Feuchy line, between the Arras-Cambrai and Neuville-Wancourt roads. On the morning of the 10th, however, news came that the *11th Division* had retired from this line further north. The divisional commander, General von Reuter, therefore ordered a withdrawal to the half-prepared Monchy village position. Screened by a snowstorm, the 350 survivors of the *163rd Regiment* fell back. They joined two companies of the centre regiment, the *162nd*, in the sunken Monchy-Guémappe road, north of the point where it crossed the Cambrai road. The reserve battalion of the *162nd* was placed on the Monchy-Roeux road, facing west and northwest, and commanding the Scarpe valley. It was the remnants of these two regiments that held up the advance of the British (37th Division) on the 10 April.'

Without reinforcements to contain the enemy attack, the situation would inevitably deteriorate, but not until the afternoon did the first arrive, advancing in artillery formation from Boiry Notre Dame, in the shape of a battalion of *3 Bavarian Division* that had been rushed from the Lille district. With divisional artillery having almost ceased to exist, the sight of a new divisional artillery crossing open ground at a gallop and unlimbering behind Monchy-le-Preux raised the defenders' spirits. As one participant recorded: 'There was a great arc of our batteries on a wide front behind our endangered positions. It was a most memorable and magnificent battle picture, lit by the evening sun.' Its timely arrival would mean a hot reception for the British attack the next day.

Casualties had been heavy after lengthy actions such as the defence of Tilloy and the holding of 3 (British) Division at the Wancourt-Feuchy line; so heavy that although units were pulled back to hold other parts of the line, it was realized that they would have to be relieved by fresher units such as *1 Battalion* of the *17 Bavarian Regiment* of *3 Bavarian Division*. The casualties of one division, *17 Reserve Division,* stand as an example of the level of loss experienced: 79 officers and 2,700 other ranks from 9-11 April.

Further proof of the intensity of the fighting is given by *11 Division*: on 9 April, it was attacked by 12 and 15 (British) Divisions and the right wing of 9 (British) Division. Fighting was severe and two battalions of *38 Regiment* were destroyed. In the centre, the front line trenches of *51 Regiment* were overrun, and the Wancourt-Feuchy line was evacuated on the morning of 10 April on the order of a staff officer, given without the approval of the divisional commander. It fell back to the new Monchy-Roeux line, and was relieved in front of Pelves by *3Bn. 125 Regiment* of *26 Division*. On the right were *10 Grenadier Regiment*, that, contrary to the general practice, had two battalions in line. 'The support companies of these battalions made a prolonged and gallant defence of the railway embankment on the 10th, but had very few survivors'. The reserve battalion, with that of *38 Regiment*, held the front from Roeux station to the Scarpe, and repulsed 4 (British) Division's attempted advance from Fampoux. Losses for *11 Division* were 105 officers and 3,154 other ranks in the two days' fighting and, of this total, British Intelligence estimates suggest 2,200 were captured.

The casualties were heavy, but the divisions had done their best – except one that had met the attack of 9 and 34 (British) Divisions, and later of 4 (British) Division; Ludendorff suggested that *14 Bavarian Division* had failed. This is a harsh judgment as even the British *Official History* implies: 'It should in fairness be said that it had received the worst of the gas bombardment, which seems to have affected its morale, in addition to the actual casualties caused. Its losses are not given, but it is known that the British took 2,800 prisoners from it. If, therefore, its ratio of prisoners to total casualties was similar to that of its neighbour, the *11th*, its losses in two days would be over 4,000.' In the same period *1 Bavarian Reserve Division* reported a loss of 112 officers and 3,021 other ranks.

The conditions made it difficult to form and man a new front. Reinforcements arrived from being in rest, from far afield places like Lille and from the general reserve; they were 'flung hurriedly into the battle-line, to be attached to divisions holding the front when the latter were still in a state to continue the struggle, and to relieve them as quickly as possible when they were not. The least mauled troops of the original front line division were left in for a longer period than those which had suffered severely and fought on, intermingled with the fresh troops. It was fortunate… that the attack became almost as disorganized as the defence', giving the defending battle-line 'time to steady itself, to consolidate new or half-prepared positions, and to put its system of ammunition supply into order.'

Continuing British pressure caused further problems. The bridgehead over the Cojeul river was held by *84* and *86 Reserve Regiments* of *18 Reserve Division;* these regiments were in danger of being cut off and the decision was made, in the evening of 11 April, by *Gruppe Arras*, to evacuate them. They withdrew in the early hours of 12 April, but the British advance guard managed to get in among them and make their withdrawal to the Guémappe-Riegel line more difficult. This new line had been hastily dug but it ran across the commanding Wancourt ridge.

Both sides have written official histories of the conflict but these do not always agree. One instance of this is the reports on the fighting for Monchy on 14 April. In the German account it was a general British attack, assisted by tanks, whereas the British report states that only two battalions without any tank support were involved. In the centre, *23rd Bavarian Regiment*, 'was broken by a "mass of British troops" from Monchy (i.e. the leading waves of two battalions). The extreme left of *18 Bavarian Regiment* swung back and took the advance in enfilade. It thereupon came to a halt, but supports "pouring out of Monchy" (which could only be the rear waves of the same two battalions) carried it forward to some 500 yards behind the original Bavarian line.' *23 Bavarian Regiment*, 'however, claims to have given way "elastically", so that the 1/R. Newfoundland and 1/Essex were caught in a trap.'

Experienced battalion and company commanders did not require orders. 'The reserve battalion of *23 Bavarian Regiment* pushed straight forward from the rear position on which it was working. The left of the *18th*, assisted by survivors of the right battalion of the 23rd, formed a barrier between Monchy and the unfortunate British troops east of it. A battalion of the *17th Bavarian Regiment* from Boiry moved up on the British right and joined hands with further surviving companies of the "elastic" 23rd. counterattacked from three sides, 150 British surrendered, but the majority tried to get back to Monchy.' This was not possible and the retreating British were shot down at leisure.

Attack was generally met with counterattack and the divisional commander, General von Wenninger, decided to attack Monchy that afternoon. The bad news arrived about 3pm when the infantry was moving up. The artillery commander reported 'that the ammunition railhead at Vitry was under heavy fire, that the destination of the trains had been altered to Corbehem, that the ammunition available was sufficient only to hold off one more big British attack, and that owing to the state of the roads the supplies could not be replenished during the night if they were expended now.' However, the history of *18 Bavarian Regiment* admits that the British placed an impenetrable barrage east of Monchy so no attack could get through. Close by, *26 Division* continued to hold its narrow front astride the Scarpe and *18 Division* its wider one between Roeux Station and the railway north of Gavrelle.

Crown Prince Rupprecht, aware that there could be further attacks, ordered a further withdrawal that was to be completed by dawn on 13 April. During the night of 11/12 April 'the remaining civilians in the villages near the third line were hurried away from their homes, and every available vehicle was used to carry back stores. The artillery withdrew, leaving only a small proportion in position. After dusk on the 12th, the front-line battalions and the last guns in action slipped away, leaving only patrols to offer a semblance of opposition to the pursuit'. As the troops were leaving, the counterattack troops were arriving with their own field artillery and the missing heavy artillery. On 18 April, these troops were to face the British 1 Corps and Canadian Corps when they attacked from the Vimy and Lorette Ridges.

The battle was not all one-sided. In an attempt to aid the Arras Front, General von Moser was given approval for a four-division attack at Lagnicourt in the Amiens – Cambrai sector. Luck was not with the troops. The attack was carried out by *2 Guard Reserve, 3 Guard, 38 Division*, and *4 Ersatz Division*, with 21 battalions in the first line. Each division was followed by two or three batteries for close support, and by parties of engineers to effect demolitions. There were hitches due to lack of preparation and knowledge of the ground, the chief result of which was that several units were very late. Little of any real significance was achieved by the attack, except by *2 Guard Reserve Division* and the *Lehr Regiment* of *3 Guard Division* on its left who took Lagnicourt at the cost of 800 men. The total casualty list for the attack was 2,313.

After 1st Scarpe came the 2nd Battle for basically the same ground. To the north of the Scarpe *161 Regiment (185 Division)*, after relieving *86 Regiment*, was attacked and driven out of Roeux by the British 51 Division; the counterattack by *86 Regiment* retook Roeux, apart from the station and chemical works, which were eventually cleared by a battalion of *65 Regiment*. A further attack, using Corps reserve troops, also failed to recover the line of the Roeux-Gavrelle road. Total losses were so severe that all the units were withdrawn and replaced by *208 Division*. The battalion in the Oppy line was destroyed by 63 Division, 'and the defence of Gavrelle then depended on a company in a quarry on the eastern side, which never reached its battle station. The reserve battalion was ordered to rally the troops who had been driven back, and retake Gavrelle, but its counterattack broke down completely'. The arrival of *185 Division* (the counterattack division) in the form of two infantry battalions marching in the open from Izel was met with heavy artillery fire and determined resistance from the British 37 and 63 Divisions on its approach to Gavrelle; a similar attempt the next morning met with the same results. The Gavrelle positions were too important not to recover and the arrival of another counterattack division in the form of *1 Guard Reserve Division* provided the opportunity for a further attempt to seize the positions; like the previous attempts nothing was gained for heavy loss, caused initially by artillery fire, and, during the attack, by machine gun fire. More successfully, to the north a number of British POWs were taken when a machine gun company fired into their attack.

Casualties during the April fighting were heavy, with total losses 'over 78,000. The sick wastage for the month numbered 1,896 officers and 49,260 other ranks. These latter figures comprise little over two and a half per cent of a force numbering, with labour units, 1,910,400'. The loss during April to the three British Armies 'engaged in the offensive, including perhaps 800 prisoners taken in the final operations against the outpost villages, were 17,959 prisoners and 254 guns; 11,295 prisoners and 185 guns by the British Third Army, 5,784 prisoners and 69 guns by the British First, and 880 prisoners by the British Fifth Army. This total of just on 18,000 prisoners in a month may be compared with the 39,000 prisoners taken by the British in the twenty weeks of the Battles of the Somme'. And so the battle continued with the 3rd Battle of the Scarpe. Attack was met with counterattack and loss of life on both sides. Although the British attacks pushed their line forward, nowhere was it conclusive, and the main structures of the Siegfried Stellung were still in place – or, if they had been dented, were replaced by new lines behind them; importantly the kingpin - the Oppy sector - was secure, however hard the fighting to take it.

According to the British *Official History*, 'the British failure was in general so complete that the defence was able to repulse the attack or drive out troops which had broken into its positions without calling upon divisions in reserve. The impression left by the accounts in regimental histories emphasizes the British infantry's lack of power of resistance when counterattacked by quite small bodies of troops'.

British casualties were high and some of the fighting was reminiscent of 1 July 1916; as then, the British 167 Brigade front held a surprise. Somehow the front-line trench of *60 Reserve Regiment (221 Division)* 'had escaped the bombardment, and the leading waves of the attack were annihilated, the Germans standing up in the open to fire into them'. Little ground was lost and many prisoners were taken. One particular incident is of note. An exhausted unit, *25 Regiment*, re-organised as one battalion, was sent back to the front along with the regimental reserves to re-take ground lost to the British 4 Division and this they duly did. The British *Official History* records what it achieved as 'a wonderful feat. counterattacking up

The winter of 1916 was both cold and wet – movement across the front was extremely difficult on both sides of the wire. The British later acknowledged that the mud was even worse than Passchendaele.

There was little or no censorship until late in 1917. Even then it was much less strict than in the British army and a soldier could say what they felt about their life or about what they had been involved in.

One of the many cemeteries lovingly tended by members of the unit. German divisions were moved around much less frequently than British ones so that proper care of the cemeteries could be maintained. Their modern-day counterparts bear little resemblence to those of 1917/1918.

the Scarpe valley, with its left on the river, its right company came unexpectedly upon a body of British troops, from which it captured 150 prisoners and three machine guns. A second party of British troops was then encountered, from which, with the aid of a detachment of the *185th Regiment*, it took fifty more prisoners. Yet another party was then overrun, so that, by the time it had re-entered Roeux and rescued a pioneer company still holding out there, it had in its hands 358 prisoners. Its own losses are given as 117. It must be added, however, that this regiment had a casualty list of just under one thousand between the 23rd April and the 3rd May.'

It was not only the British who were attacking; the whole purpose of the British attacks had been to take the focus to the Arras front so that the main attack could occur on the Chemin des Dames. The start of both offensives was pre-empted by an attack on French positions. After a violent artillery bombardment on 4 April, an attack was launched on a front of three and a half miles, with the right flank on Sapigneul, just south of the Aisne. Initially successful, attaining the Aisne-Marne Canal, 700 yards behind the French line, in the centre of the attack zone French counterattacks gradually recovered the lost ground; by 12 April almost the whole of it was again in French hands. However, while no territory was gained, the attack plans for the French offensive were captured. Although General Nivelle knew about the loss by 7 April, two days before the launch of the British offensive, he decided that the operations already scheduled would continue.

Although the French hid their intentions, new fortifications were under way in the shape of the Hunding Stellung and the Brunhild Stellung, with considerable further work being done to turn a slender fortified zone into an exceptionally strong one. 'Fresh divisions were brought in, from the "pool" created by the withdrawal; the heavy artillery was reinforced; large reserves of munitions were amassed. The Crown Prince established at Sedan a Senior Officers' School – similar to that of *Prince Rupprecht's Army Group* at Valenciennes – for instruction in the new principles of the *Abwehrschlacht*, or defensive battle. Some training of the troops was also possible, and the pause afforded by the withdrawal' notably improved morale. There were 21 divisions in the front line, with 17 in reserve against 53 French divisions.

Due to bad weather conditions the French attack was postponed until 16 April for the G.A.R. and that of the G.A.C. to the next day. 'On many parts of the front, however, it appeared that the breaches made in the wire defences were not complete or had been repaired, and it was evident to the most optimistic that the infantry had a heavy task before it'.

The morning started misty with an overclouded sky and almost from the start it was evident that the preparation had been incomplete. Under an often light counter-barrage, the French troops advanced into heavy machine gun fire; there were many casualties and, where any success was gained the French positions soon met with counterattacks. Later in the day French troops in the bigger penetrations faced full-scale counterattacks which French tanks pushed forward and helped beat off. But in most cases the infantry were too exhausted to keep up. Tank losses were high, particularly to the west of the Miette river, where the French tanks were observed leaving the Bois de Beau Marais and bombarded by artillery, with twenty-three being destroyed before they reached the front line.

On the Chemin des Dames ridge even less progress was made by the French, and all that remained in French control by evening was the support line, two or three hundred yards behind the front. The French 'losses had been very heavy and hardly a division was capable of another serious effort. Where the attack had been most successful, it was still short of the line which it was to have reached by 9.30 a.m. On the other hand, a very large haul of prisoners, over 7,000, had been captured'. The story was the same all along the attack front and the breakthrough promised to the French troops had not been achieved, although there was success the next day when the French Sixth Army continued its attacks and, by keeping up steady pressure, forced the voluntary abandonment of the defence triangle Braye-Condé-Laffaux where many guns (some undamaged) and large amounts of munitions were left behind. Although the maximum advance by 20 April was only four miles, the French had taken 20,000 prisoners and 147 guns, freed the railway from Soissons to Reims, taken the Aisne valley west of the Oise – Aisne Canal and the second position south of Juvincourt, along with some of the most important peaks in Champagne. However, resolute defence had made the French losses very heavy – over 96,000 by 25 April, and, although the loss of defending troops was less, it was still very high at over 83,000. The German High Command claimed it as a victory because the French had not broken through, but the fighting men on both sides knew it was a victory for no one. In French political circles, any success there had been was nullified by a disappointment that turned it into a failure, looked upon with anger, disillusionment and horror; heads had to roll and a number of Generals were replaced, including Nivelle.

Even so the French offensive was continued for a considerable time with some large scale attacks producing only a very limited amount of success, including the capture of the Californie plateau and the capture of the Hindenburg Line on a two and a half mile front on the Chemin des Dames ridge that bit deeply into the salient opposite Laffaux. The total losses to the French up to 10 May were approximately 28,500 prisoners and 187 guns.

The failure of the Nivelle offensive had a further effect towards the end of May – mutiny. Unfortunately the German High Command did not believe the reports of a French troop mutiny until it was too late to use the information. One soldier, P C Ettinger, who was in the Front Line trenches, recorded in his memoirs that in early June, about 2.30 a.m., 'three escaped German prisoners of war came over No Man's Land. The escort detailed to take them back learnt from them – and the story ran like wildfire along the front – that they had been wandering in the French lines for nearly a fortnight, and that there was trouble there. Whole divisions had mutinied, regiments had left their positions, flying the red flag. They want to make an end of the War, one way or another. The French army is tired. The rumours about a mutiny in the French army ceased after a few days. Too wild to be true. No trace of a possibility was the verdict. The escaped prisoners wanted to tell a good story and make themselves important'.

OHL was unaware that there had been 119 cases of collective indiscipline recorded, of which 80 were classed as serious. 'Typical acts of indiscipline were manifestations against the War, stone-throwing, and window-breaking, with some incendiarism. Refusal to go into the line was common, but attacks on officers were very rare. Starting a little later, there were grave incidents in the leave trains, the first taking place at Troyes on the 19th May and the critical period being from the 6th to the 27th June. There were displays of red flags, singing of revolutionary songs, uncoupling of engines, mishandling of military police and railway servants. It was estimated that more than half the leave men returned in a state of drunkenness'.

Third Ypres

Although the French troops were prepared to defend their lines they would not attack. As a result of the unreliability of the French Army during this period the British offensive at Arras would have to continue in order to conceal this problem, and when Arras finally did finish, the focus would move to the Flanders plain and a further British offensive – Third Ypres. The British *Official History* recorded that 'the campaign was fought by Sir Douglas Haig, on a front favourable on account of its strategic advantages, in order to prevent the Germans falling upon the French Armies, shaken and dispirited after three years of unceasing warfare and finally mutinous in consequence of the losses in and failure of the Nivelle offensive, upon which such great hopes had been set'. However, OHL received information from a spy that there would be an attack in the Ypres area so that there would be no surprise when it came. This was further corroborated by information from prisoners taken on the Arras front; 'statements of prisoners proved conclusively that no further big attacks were to be expected in the Arras sector, and that a big attack was to take place from the Armentieres-Ypres front about the 7th June, after an eight-day bombardment'.

The Battle of Passchendaele, as it is more popularly called, achieved many of its targets but is now generally seen as a pointless bloodbath for British troops. Whatever one's point of view on this battle, the German view was that it had a serious effect upon morale, spirit and the number of reserves. Crown Prince Rupprecht initially thought of a withdrawal from the Flanders front but with the arrival of the October rain things changed, although he also records: 'Our troops are steadily deteriorating'. Health was certainly deteriorating: 'Owing to the constant rain and the exertions of bringing up ammunition, rations

General Ludendorff, the driving force behind the German Army on the Western Front.

Westlicher Kriegsschauplatz.
Grabenstellung von rückwärts.

A frontline trench in eastern France during the winter of 1916.

The remains of Chaulnes during the withdrawal to the Seigfreid Line.

Hendecourt during the withdrawal – nearly everything of use to the Allies was destroyed in the withdrawal.

and water through the mud, there was much sickness, and nearly everyone had diarrhoea.' There were also problems with discipline: 'as early as July marauding and thieving were rife and, if the field gendarmerie interfered, the soldiers made short business of the gendarmes'. This view is reflected in a post-war General Staff publication which stated that this battle brought the German Army near to destruction and compelled an attack in 1918 as the last chance of victory.

The cost of this offensive was summed up by Crown Prince Rupprecht's Order of the Day of 5 December 1917: '88 divisions (22 of them twice), the mass of the artillery reserve and other arms and formations of the central reserve have taken part in this, the most prodigious of all battles so far fought. Divisions disappeared by dozens into the turmoil of the battle, only to emerge from the witches' cauldron after a short period, thinned and exhausted, often reduced to a miserable remnant, and the gaping spaces left by them were filled by fresh divisions'. In corroboration General Kuhl wrote that 'the hell of Verdun was surpassed' and that this battle was known in Germany as 'the greatest martyrdom of the World War' and that 'the Flanders battle consumed the German strength to such a degree that the harm done could no longer be repaired. The sharp edge of the German sword had become jagged. And the morale of the German nation was broken. . . In millions of letters from the Western Front, from April to November, came an ever-rising number of bitter complaints of the almost unbearable hardships and bloody losses in the scarcely interrupted chain of battles: Arras, Aisne-Champagne [Nivelle], Flanders, Verdun and the Chemin des Dames, Malmaison. A hundred thousand leave men told the Home Front by word of mouth the details of the ever-growing superiority of the enemy, particularly in weapons of destruction'.

One negative effect of the British preparations was to remove troops from the French sector, where it would have been possible to attack the weakened French divisions who were still coming to terms with the failure of the Nivelle offensive and the mutinies that followed. The Crown Prince proposed an attack in strength across the Aisne, opposite Paris, that required thirty divisions, but as only twenty-three were available and eight of these were scheduled to move north to counter British intentions, the plan was not feasible. The British preparations therefore stopped an attack on a front that was held by only two reliable French divisions; it also indirectly affected the campaign of 1918 in that its casualty rate meant there were no replacements, apart from the class of 1899 (eighteen-year-olds) and recovered sick and wounded. This state of affairs was not replicated on the British side.

Before the start of Third Ypres came the Messines Ridge battle that moved the front line back in a very successful, quick and limited sized attack. At 0310 hours on 7 June, nineteen great mines exploded in 'leaping streams of orange flames, nineteen gigantic roses with carmine petals...which rose up slowly and majestically out of the ground'. So great was the shock, that, in occupied Lille, fifteen miles behind the line, soldiers rushed in panic into the streets'.

In April, Lieutenant Colonel Fusslein, officer in charge of mining operations in the Messines area, had reported to his superiors that 'a subterranean attack by mine-explosions on a large scale beneath the front line to precede an infantry assault against the Messines Ridge was no longer possible', but three weeks later he had changed his mind and, even though other senior officers asked for the front line to be very thinly held in case of attack, little notice was taken of the potential danger from mines.

The battle report of *204 Division*, holding the sector, stated that 'the ground trembled as in a natural earthquake, heavy concrete shelters rocked, a hurricane of hot air from the explosions swept back for many kilometres, dropping fragments of wood, iron and earth; and gigantic black clouds of smoke and dust spread over the country. The effect on the troops was overpowering and crushing'.

In the battle zone, while the earth was still shaking, the enemy attacked an unnerved garrison. Over a large area outpost groups were killed, wounded or stunned, allowing the British troops to penetrate the defences quickly. Further back, many troops ran away in panic whilst others cowered in defeat in shell holes and derelict shelters while 80,000 enemy troops advanced. After a week the Messines Salient had been lost to the British assault. The German *Official History* gives five principal reasons for the loss of the Messines-Wytschaete Ridge: 'the great numerical superiority of the British in artillery, aircraft and infantry and the thorough preparatory work; the effect of the mine explosions, both in number and size beyond any precedent; the unfavourable infantry position on the long forward slope; the cramped deployment area for the supporting artillery within the salient which could be enfiladed from both flanks; and, lastly, the late arrival of the Eingreif divisions on the battlefield'.

Before the start of the enemy offensive, the army was 680,000 stronger than in the autumn of 1916 but now the army was haemorrhaging; in the months April to June on the Western Front alone, losses stood at 384,000, of whom 121,000 were listed as killed or missing. Additionally, munitions were sufficient only for defensive action.

The Crown Prince wanted to mount his own offensive but was mindful of the shortage of artillery shells. However, the Head of Operations Staff suggested a limited attack against the recently arrived British divisions in the Nieuport Sector; this he felt would help disorganise enemy preparations for their offensive. A suggestion of a further operation south of the Menin Road – to disorganise British artillery preparations - was turned down. Surprise was of the essence but a prisoner of *3 Marine Regiment*, captured on 5 April, by the British, 'stated that a British attack was expected shortly and that reinforcements of German artillery were being brought up. Two raids carried out on the night of the 9th/10th succeeded in capturing a prisoner, but he was killed by a shell soon afterwards, so this possible source of information of the German attack also failed'. British aerial reconnaissance also failed to spot the intended attack.

From 6 July to 10 July an intermittent bombardment fell on the British positions, 'on the wooden pontoons across the Yser, on the trenches and dug-outs on the sandy beaches and on the sparse gun lines in the rear', but it was not enough of a bombardment to arouse the suspicion of an attack among the British troops. At 20.00 hours on 10 July, fifteen battalions, in five waves, led by a storm unit of the Marine Corps, attacked towards the right bank of the Yser and rapidly captured it on the seaward side of Lombardsijde; the attack to this point took twenty minutes and was carefully orchestrated. 'The first wave, consisting of groups of a specially trained assault detachment, advanced straight through to the back, or third, British breastwork, cleared it, and, after a pause of ten minutes, pressed on to the bank of the Yser; the second wave cleared the dug-outs of the second breastwork and then occupied the third breastwork; the third wave reinforced the first wave and established an outpost system along the river bank, placing machine guns to command the river; the fourth, carrying material for consolidating the position, cleared the dug-outs of the first breastwork and followed on to the third; the fifth occupied and held the second breastwork'. However, the British 32 Division succeeded in regaining all but 500 yards of its positions. The successful attack cost the enemy defenders 126 officers and 3,000 other ranks.

From dominating observation areas, the British preparations for the battle were obvious and indeed the British *Official History* called the Flanders campaign of 1917 'the most clearly heralded offensive of the war'. For two months, observation and aerial reconnaissance showed the British troops constructing hutments, gun emplacements, roads and tramways, indicated the arrival of new divisions, the supplies that would be needed and artillery reinforcements.

By 12 June, 'Crown Prince Rupprecht of Bavaria, commanding the Northern Group of German Armies, described a British offensive in Flanders as certain' and on 13 June Colonel von Lossberg, the defensive battle expert, was brought in to build up the defensive positions: 'a deeper defence, no deep dug-outs, and counterattack by special reserve divisions which were to be close up, that is in the zone of enemy long-range fire, so that they, in case of need, could at once be engaged'.

Using the new doctrine, the defensive positions would consist of three zones (forward, battle and rearward) each 2,000-3,000 yards deep, 'the backs of which were marked by the Second (Albrecht), the Third (Wilhelm) and the Flanders Line, respectively. Heavy casualties in the preliminary bombardment would be avoided by holding the forward line thinly and an enemy assault was to be broken up by local counterattacks using the supports and reserves of the battalions holding the position. Any further enemy advance would be countered by the belt of strong points and fortified localities behind the front line.

The whole process of defence had been clearly thought out with the second line protecting the field artillery and providing shelters for reserve troops. Behind them were further reserves who were ready to counterattack when the enemy started to lose momentum. In the rearward zone waited the specially organized counterattack divisions, one to each two frontline divisions; each counterattack division having one regiment – three battalions – immediately available to assist the frontline division and two further regiments held in reserve further back. Behind them were further reserve divisions. Unfortunately the amount of labour and quantity of material required for the construction of the Hindenburg and Wotan positions up to 'early June had limited work on the Flanders Positions, so that by the end of July only the forward zone was complete, with concrete battery emplacements farther back' with a number of farm ruins in the battle zone converted into centres of resistance. Although the defences were incomplete, Colonel Lossberg gave OHL an assurance 'that the co-operation of infantry and artillery, and the immediate participation of the counterattack divisions, had been thoroughly prepared'. To add further evidence for the readiness to counter any British offensive, Crown Prince Rupprecht confidently 'recorded that he had ample forces and ammunition to meet the coming offensive'; an indiscreet speech by Painlevé, the French War Minister, making it clear that French assistance for the attack would be of only a limited character, further boosted his confidence in the outcome.

However, the extended barrage had had its effect. Moving off behind their barrage at 03.50 hours on 31 July, the assaulting enemy battalions of the British Second Army found the wire well cut and the defenders of the forward zone either disabled, ready to surrender or in flight; those defenders who did fight were quickly overcome and by noon the front line had moved back by 1,000 yards. Further north on Fifth Army Front, the resistance slowed down the British advance and inflicted considerable casualties but in places it penetrated to 2,000 yards. In most cases the British assault had not got further than the first line of the defences so there was no need to use the assault divisions, except in the sector between the Ypres-Roulers railway and St. Julien where the British had breached the third trench line. Here *50 Reserve Division*, a counterattack division of *Gruppe Ypres*, successfully pushed back the attacking troops to the previous defensive line. However, by the end of 2 August, most of the first and second defence lines had been lost to the British and the battle was to continue through sun, rain and mud into November in two further phases.

By 3 August, although the attackers had not reached all of their objectives, they had seized the important heights on Gheluvelt plateau and the long rise via Bellewaarde to Pilckem, thus denying observation of their movements. Nine divisions were badly mauled by the attacks and the front line divisions had to be replaced with fresh divisions. Losses were heavy in men and materiel, including over 6,000 POWs and twenty-five field guns; fresh divisions arrived from other areas depleting the defences whence they came, and large quantities of heavy ammunition were sent from positions on the French front. Between 25 July and 28 August, twenty-three divisions out of the thirty deployed on the enemy's Fifth Army front alone were withdrawn as exhausted. General von Kuhl, Chief of the General Staff on the Front, spoke of the campaign as 'the greatest martyrdom of the World War' and stated that 'no division could stick it out in this hell for more than fourteen days. It must then be relieved. . . Foot and bowel complaints ravaged the troops.'

By September the front line had moved no more than 4,000 yards back - less at essential points – and had caused the enemy nearly 70,000 casualties. The artillery, still commanding the slight but decisive heights, had the ability to choose targets of opportunity deep within the attackers' rear area, making reinforcement and supply difficult for the enemy. The British had failed to gain artillery superiority – an essential in trench offensives.

Although the British were being checked, it was not a German victory and, even though many of the counterattacks succeeded, Ludendorff wrote in his memoirs that '31st July 1917 till well into September was a period of tremendous anxiety. . .The fighting on the Western Front became more serious than any the German army had yet experienced. On 31st July the fighting caused us very heavy losses in prisoners and stores, and a large expenditure of reserves; and the costly August battles imposed a great strain on the Western troops. The state of affairs in the West appeared to prevent the execution of our plans elsewhere. Our wastage had been so high as to cause grave misgivings, and exceeded all our expectations'. He also complained that the counterattack divisions arrived too late to catch the attackers when they were at their weakest and that the enemy had quickly adapted to the use of the counterattack division.

As a result of the attacks, it was decided to hold back the counterattack divisions on the day of assault and engage them only on the following day in a systematic counterattack. This naturally depended upon the frontline divisions having 'sufficient fighting power to stop the first onrush of the enemy at the line of main resistance'. It was decided to strengthen the front line by giving them more machine guns from back areas and the support positions; battalions in the support positions were also to be 'pushed to the front as soon as, or before, the battle began, so as to catch the enemy whilst consolidating'. Finally, each counterattack division was to send up one battalion behind each regiment of a front line division, as far as the artillery protection position. This was a return to the pre-war system that provided one solid line of defence.

Further defensive decisions were laid out on 22 September. 'There must be increased artillery counter-preparation before the battle; more offensive raids to make the enemy strengthen his front lines and incur loss; strengthening of artillery observation in the battle area, so that fire would be effective when the enemy entered it; and the speeding up of the counterattacks'.

Although the British artillery continued to pound the German positions, there was a pause in the fighting during the middle of October as the British Army replaced worn-out divisions with new units, while on the German side it was becoming ever more difficult to find reserves. Heavy fighting started again in the last fortnight of October, continuing through to 6 November, when Passchendaele village was captured by the Canadians. By 10 November the battle was over.

As the battle had continued with ever more complex attack and barrage arrangements, the casualties mounted. By the end of the year, *Fourth Army*, which had borne the brunt of the attack, put its losses between 21 July and 31 December at 217,000, of whom 35,000 were killed and 48,000 missing with the loss of 26,631 men as prisoners.

The Battle of Cambrai

The Cambrai sector formed part of the front of the *Second Army* (General von der Marwitz) on the left of Crown Prince Rupprecht's Group of Armies in an area that had become known as the 'Flanders sanatorium'. The area was garrisoned by lower grade troops and used as a resting area for battle-weary troops from the Ypres sector and convalescing units. The defensive positions contained many captured field guns and ammunition was short, but the whole Hindenburg position was regarded as strong and it was expected that the preliminary destructive bombardment would give ample warning.

From 10 November onwards, foggy weather put air reconnaissance out of the question but, even without this valuable information, the Army commander in the area reported to Crown Prince Rupprecht's headquarters, on 16 November, that 'hostile attacks on a large scale against the Army front are not to be expected in the near future'. However, by this time some suspicion had been aroused, even though no information was obtained by the prisoners captured in the raids on 20 and 55 British Divisions. The interrogation of those prisoners taken from 36 British Division in the early morning of 18 November revealed that an attack in the Havrincourt sector was in preparation, but that the date of the attack was not clear. Reporting to OHL on the same day, Crown Prince Rupprecht deduced that there would be partial attacks on various other parts of the front by the British.

Further suspicion was aroused by the number of British aeroplanes that flew low over the lines on 19 November, and infantry and artillery observers who detected unusual activity on the British side. 'The fragment of a telephone message: 'Tuesday flanders...' was picked up by a listening station at Riencourt' so the area was accordingly reinforced by one regiment and some field batteries from Army reserve. The defensive strength of *Gruppe Caudry* was further strengthened by the arrival of *107 Division* (Major-General Havenstein) from Russia as a replacement for *20 Landwehr Division* (a low fighting capacity division). That same night an order was issued at midnight that an attack, probably using tanks, was

One occupation that showed no sign of decreasing – erecting memorials to the fallen. Considerable effort and expense was taken over many of them, particularly divisional cemeteries.

A view of French held territory in the eastern part of France.

The Kaiser, Hindenburg and Ludendorff at their HQ in January 1917.

expected in the Havrincourt sector; *Gruppe Arras* issued a similar order, and expected that the four-to-five-hours' preliminary bombardment would probably begin between 2.00am and 3.00am (German time).

At 06.20 hours 20 November, led by their commander, General Elles, who was flying his flag in one of the leading machines, 381 British tanks moved forward from their assembly points. The wire was easily crushed, troops fled in terror and a hole was torn in the Siegfried Stellung almost six miles wide and up to 4,000 yards deep. The surprise was complete: confusion and local panic resulted in one officer later recording that 'some of the infantry seemed to be off their heads with fright', but by the afternoon the troops were generally fighting well. On the Flesquières sector, the strongest sector opposite the British IV Corps, the advance was checked; this ultimately ruined the effectiveness of the battle. Here the greatest number of tanks were disabled by gunners who had been trained to fire at moving targets; moreover, in some sectors, anti-aircraft guns mounted on lorries proved very effective against tanks. Losses for the day included over 4,000 POWs and 100 guns but, by the afternoon, much of the loss had been made good by the arrival of fresh divisions from other parts of the front. But, as General von der Marwitz reported to his superior, there would not be enough men available for a counterattack before 27 November.

Fortunately, the British were also surprised by the extent of their success; their momentum slowed down due to exhaustion and lack of supplies. The arrival of fresh troops and the launching of counterattacks pushed the enemy back in many places, but the offensive continued in the Bourlon sector and there it became an infantry slogging match. The battle for the village and wood was ferocious, especially on 24 November, when it looked likely that the enemy might take the village. However, by 11.00 hours, only one small segment of the British attacking force was still there - it stayed there for a further two days. On 24 November, 'the Commander-in-Chief issued a Special Order of the Day thanking commanders and all ranks of all arms and services for their exertions, and congratulating them on the success so far achieved: 'The capture of the important Bourlon position yesterday crowns a most successful operation and opens the way to a further exploitation of the advantages already gained'.

The defenders had one final attack to face on 27 November, when two divisions and thirty tanks advanced against the Bourlon and Fontaine sectors. Casualties on both sides were heavy and a ten-battalion counterattack drove one of the British divisions back to its start line. After this the British Third Army closed down its offensive and put up defensive wire.

While the British positions in Bourlon Wood were being quite heavily shelled, the rest of the front was menacingly quiet on both 28 and 29 November when preparations for the counterattack were underway. Although Rupprecht regarded the recapture of the Hindenburg front system as the minimum to be achieved, plans for a greater advance were drawn up. The enemy, he observed, 'must have been aware of increased movement and activity during the last days of November, but nothing was done to disturb the preparations. The night of the 29th/30th November was a quiet one and the assembly was not interfered with by any hostile action'.

The attack plan envisaged a short, intense bombardment followed by a rapid attack by *Gruppe Caudry* and *Gruppe Busigny*. At 08.30 hours on 30 November an intense bombardment fell on the new British positions; a counter-offensive had started as one sergeant in 1 Royal Berkshires reported to his officer: 'SOS gone up in twenty-seven different places, and the Bosche coming over the (h)ill in thousands'. The British were aware of the possibility of a counterattack and one unit had issued the order: 'In the event of attack you will hold the line at all costs. There is to be no retirement to any second line'. The style of the attack was novel on the Western Front; behind the intense and short bombardment the infantry were to advance in groups employing infiltration tactics that ignored strong points and moved forward on the line of least resistance. To aid the progress of the front units, artillery batteries were to advance immediately behind the infantry, with close support being provided by low-flying aircraft that were to bomb and strafe enemy positions.

The speed of the attack took many British units completely by surprise and two generals were nearly captured because of the rapid penetration. However, the troops in the vanguard were insufficiently trained in the new method of attack and with heavy officer losses there was a lack of control. As a result of ever increasing enemy resistance and counterattacks, the German attack did not progress at the initial speed in all sectors. Ernst Jünger, a Leutnant in *73 Hanover Fusilier Regiment,* later wrote about the intensity of the fighting: 'We then entered the trench on the right. It was full of arms and equipment and English dead…going further we met with resolute resistance.'

After forty-eight hours, the troops and horses were exhausted and ammunition was in short supply; orders called a halt, with the next day to be devoted to consolidation, and forward positions being organized as an outpost zone. Regardless of this, the moral effect on the troops who had been on the defensive for so long was a very beneficial one.

On 3 December, the attack continued with the capture of La Vacquerie and the withdrawal of the enemy from the east bank of the St. Quentin Canal. Responding to the situation the next day, the British withdrew from the Bourlon salient and, by 7 December, Bourlon Wood, the Marcoing area and long stretches of the Siegfried Stellung had been retaken; while Havrincourt, Flesquières and Ribécourt remained in enemy hands, much territory southwest of Welsh Ridge had been taken and in many places the enemy were back at the start line of the offensive. However, although little real gain had been achieved by either side, both had learned valuable lessons for the coming year: 'Our action has given us valuable hints for an offensive battle in the west if we wished to undertake one in 1918', wrote Hindenburg in his memoirs and, as Rupprecht recorded, 'It was our biggest success over the British since 1915 at Ypres' and 'captures from the British, since the opening of the counter-offensive had amounted to 75 officers, 2,556 other ranks and 85 guns'. However, the enemy had taken 189 officers, 10,916 other ranks and ninety-eight guns.

Although the offensive had finished, there was continued fighting; part of *16 Bavarian Division* had a limited success in a local attack on 12 December near Bullecourt and there were further successes at Messines and Polderhoek.

Both sides took stock of the situation and made plans for the coming year. On the enemy side there were large numbers of Americans arriving every week, but British troops were not being sent out in the numbers needed; Russia had finally given in, freeing tens of thousands of troops for active service on the Western Front. One bonus was that much had been learned about combating the tank, and rules were laid out to combat the threat: ground was to be reconnoitered with a view to its suitability for tank action and heavy bridges were to be replaced by lighter ones unable to bear a tank's weight; steel rails set at a forward angle in concrete would act as tank stops, while village streets were to be barricaded with heavy vehicles to stop the progress of a tank. Infantry and machine guns were to be disposed in groups, well hidden and using armour-piercing bullets to hit the vulnerable parts of the tank; light trench mortars were to be well dug in, in order to obtain a flat trajectory: bunches of hand grenades could be thrown on to the roof of a tank. Very importantly, fire discipline was to be strictly enforced, with infantry taking cover during a tank assault; they were only to emerge when the following infantry were close by, with close support being provided by aircraft.

The die was cast. With the release of first-class troops from the eastern front, 1918 would be the final throw of the dice: a gamble that had to be taken. Germany must win the war before the full entry of American forces onto the Western Front, and before grim despondency turned into defeatism.

A guard post, near a cross road, in a quiet area well behind the lines.

A knocked-out British tank on the Arras front.

The effect of British 'drumfire' on a trench.

Even though there was a battle waging in Flanders there was still time to send an Easter greetings card.

Although quality control in British munitions factories had improved there was still a large number of dud shells. This photo was taken during the Arras offensive and shows three sizes of British shells.

Lunch break in the trenches.

A minenwerfer being loaded during the Arras battle.

Life in the trenches was mentally and physically exhausting so any time there was for sleeping was taken, regardless of where it was.

The photographer calls to capture a moment for the folks back home. As with letters home, there was little censorship of photographs.

The main street in Vimy before the Arras offensive. After the attack the village was a ruin.

Trenches in a mine crater on the Arras front – note the moveable barbed wire fortifications.

The town square in Monchy before the 1917 attacks.

Monchy bei·Arras.
Marktplatz.

Heavy artillery in Willerval, well behind the lines on the Arras front.

Most material was moved to the front using horse-drawn wagons as petrol was more scarce than for the Allied forces.

In the front line at Oppy on 28 April. The positions around Oppy were crucial and were not taken until the end of the war.

An aggressive stance for the camera, with each soldier carrying a hand grenade in his belt. The German hand grenade was an offensive weapon that created a lot of noise and smoke but was not at lethal as the British Mills bomb.

The result of a direct hit – trench mortars were constantly moved around because they attracted the attention of enemy artillery.

Gefangene Engländer aus den Kämpfen vor Arras in einem Sammellager hinter der Front.

Although it was a British offensive there was a considerable number of British prisoners taken.

Transport in the flooded Oise plain during the Arras offensive.

As the war lengthened, more and more use was made of telephone communication even though it could be picked up by the enemy. A soldier stands outside the telephone bunker.

Clearing the wounded from the battlefield.

A battlefield scene on the western front.

The effect of high explosive.

Artillery spotting out of view from the enemy.

A German POW with his guards in one of the many POW camps in France.

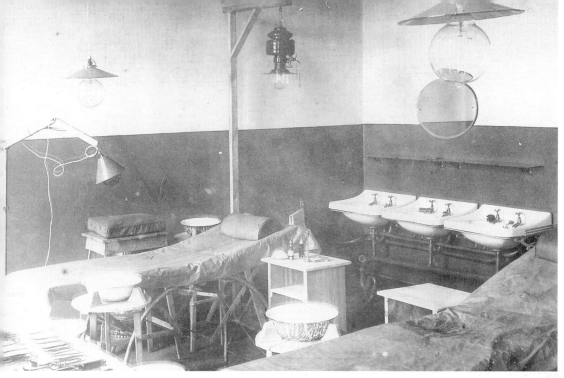

An operating theatre in 1917.

First things first – the morning wash for troops on rest – Morgen-toilette

Morgen-Toilette

Drawing water from the village well; most of the civilians left in the villages were women.

The withdrawal to the Seigfreid Stellung.

An artist's interpretation of the battle for Roeux in April 1917.

Troops practising the attack.

Wearing gas masks was uncomfortable and hindered the work of the artillery.

French troops captured in early 1917 make their way to the rear in open railway wagons.

German machine guns were heavy and had to be carried on a special sleigh.

Maschinengewehre rücken zur Verstärkung vor.

A 587

Feindlicher Graben nach dem Sturm.

French casualties litter the ground after an attack.

The lack of steel helmets among the captors suggests that this photo of French prisoners was taken well behind the front line.

Whenever possible conditions underground were made as comfortable as possible – this is an officer's room complete with mirror and covered walls and ceiling prop.

A quality trench – wooden-floored and iron-gated.

Rest and relaxation out of the sound of gunfire – 'skinny dipping' in a French river.

Making the most of the good weather – an office outside. The soldier with the bicycle is responsible for delivering messages to other units.

Well behind the front, soldiers sort the mail – mail was important in keeping up morale and in providing contact between home and the front.

Gone are the days of plenty in the commissary; now all that was left for sale were tobacco products.

Marching through town on their way to the front, the soldiers are watched by young boys wearing sabots; leather was a thing of the past.

An underground communications room during a quiet period.

An artillery observation post.

Lice were endemic on the Western Front; hunting them was a source of much amusement.

Troops helping prepare the ground for crops – relationships between occupiers and occupied were not always completely negative.

Newly-dug reserve positions

The ruins of Messines after the fighting.

Reserve positions near the Belgian coast. In quieter areas such positions could develop into considerable constructions.

Troops of the 2nd Marine Division in Belgium.

Marine Division machine gunners in Belgium. Like the British Royal Naval Division, the Marine Division troops were an elite force.

There may have been a war on but there was still time for fun; an Aunt Sally for the troops to vent their aggression on.

A British position after the Nieuport attack.

British POWs taken after the coastal battles in July 1917.

Life underground complete with home comforts.

Troops integrated into village life wherever possible. Here an older soldier looks after the cows.

German dead.

A church service in the second line trenches.

The flooded areas of Belgium; many areas of Belgium had been deliberately flooded in 1914 to stop the German advance.

105mm field artillery piece damaged on 16 April 1917 during the Arras battles.

Troop entertainment well
behind the front line.

Results of the British bombardment of the church of
St Peter and Paul in Ostend on 22 September 1917.

An unknown activity in a quiet
area. Note the remains of a British
tank in the background – probably
on the Arras front.

While many of the prisoners captured by the British were sent back to Britain, some were kept in France to act as labourers. Here they are taking a rest between felling trees and producing planks for the front.

Captured French trench mortar shells.

A newly dug-in mortar of *9 Reserve Artillery Regiment.*

Cambrai in late 1917.

The large scale use of tanks at Cambrai resulted in initially dramatic advances and also large losses in tanks. A knocked-out British tank that could be repaired for use against its original owners.

Captured British tank of 3 Battalion (the letter indicates the number of the battalion, the number is the tank number indicating the tank is from 9 Company, 10 Section). Another tank that is in good enough condition to be returned to service. Note the anti-German painting at the rear of the tank.

The main street in Fontaine near Cambrai, with another captured and repairable tank

The German view of No Man's Land during winter 1917.

British prisoners arrive at their new home in Germany after the Battle of Cambrai.

A comfortable and warm billet in Germany for those who had been wounded.

German Marine soldiers in the trenches in Flanders.

The demand of the army for soldiers was never ending – more youthful recruits in training.

In the Quartermaster's stores – supplies of new uniforms to replace those damaged in the day-to-day existence of life at the front.

A mature soldier of *81 Regiment* serving in *41 Ersatz* (false) *Regiment* of *8 Ersatz Division* - Ersatz units were created for specific needs from surplus troops.

Having fun behind the lines – officers and senior NCOs playing in a frozen ditch.

Better than winter in the trenches – potentially comfortable billets well behind the lines.

Chapter Two

1918

On 11 November 1917, Ludendorff presided at a conference in Mons to discuss how a decision could be forced in the west. The conclusion that was reached was that neither the Russian nor Italian front would affect the ability of the army to deliver a major assault. The attack should be at the end of February or beginning of March. Most importantly, it must be against the British; if the British Army (the dominant partner) was broken, the French Army would capitulate.

Ludendorff was aware of his limited manpower reserve and knew that his forces must therefore rely upon tactical skill, not sheer weight of numbers, and that brain-power must overcome the enemy's strength. He issued decrees that all troops must undergo special offensive training in accordance with the new handbook, 'The Attack in Trench Warfare'. Newly arrived divisions from the east passed through the new instructional centres who trained soldiers, both officers and men, before these divisions were assigned to a sector. Units already on the front were combed for their fittest, most experienced and youngest soldiers, who were then trained and formed into *Sturmabteilungen* – the storm troops; in high quality units the reverse happened: less able soldiers were sent to other units, often on the Eastern Front, where they replaced the more able soldiers sent west.

The *Sturmabteilungen* were the elite of the army. They carried flamethrowers, light machineguns and light trench mortars. Their role in the attack was to cross enemy trench lines and bypass pockets of heavy resistance, such as machine gun posts, and attack artillery positions. Their purpose was infiltration at the fastest possible speed.

Following behind them were 'battle units' - engineers, infantry, machine gunners, trench mortar teams, along with field artillery sections and ammunition carriers, trained to attack defended positions and repulse counterattacks. As with the *Sturmabteilungen*, speed was paramount, and any position they could not take was to be left for the following waves to deal with. Similarly, tanks were to be ignored and left for the troops following behind them, but any following enemy infantry were to be dealt with on sight. Any breakthrough that was achieved was to be re-inforced by reserves, rather than, as had been usual, employing these where the battle was held up.

By the day of the attack the British positions would be faced by over $3^1/_2$ million soldiers, forming 194 divisions, of which sixty-seven were facing thirty-three enemy divisions. Secrecy was paramount. All important and large-scale troop movements should be carried out at night; no troop train could unload unless there were arrangements to disperse the men immediately. 'Safety Officers' controlled all means of communication and censored the mail. Any officer who knew any detail of the attack was sworn to secrecy. Secrecy was taken a stage further with the use of police aircraft and balloons to camouflage and search for any new tracks left by moving men and equipment. However, the possibility of an attack was deduced by the British from statements they took from deserters and from their reconnaissance flights that showed the construction of large ammunition dumps and light railways. The date of the attack was a well-kept secret until 18 March, when a German pilot who had been shot down revealed the date as either 20 or 21 March. When, on 19 March, this was corroborated by German prisoners and deserters, the only questions still in doubt on the British side were 'whether the first attack would be the main effort or merely a preparatory one, and whether or not the French would be attacked simultaneously.' So confident were the British that General Gough wrote home that night that he expected the bombardment would start on the night of 20 March, last between six and eight hours and be followed by

Troops on the Eastern Front. In a few month's time those who were either young, fit or seasoned veterans would be moved to the Western Front for the coming offensives.

A simple way of listening to the enemy but rather difficult to transport about in No Mans Land.

Part of the staff of 7. (Würtemmberg) Landwehr-Div. – many of whom would soon find themselves serving on the Western Front.

German infantry on 21 March; he was only a few hours early with his prediction.

The most secret parts of the plan were the artillery preparations conducted by Colonel Bruchmüller, an advocate of surprise and of the use of gas shells prior to the attack. It had been difficult to move men, but it was far more so to move batteries of artillery, and elaborate plans to move the guns were employed with the final batteries arriving just before they were due to go into action. To further increase the surprise, there were to be no registration shots on a given target. Any firing would rely upon a mathematical prediction of range and bearing, a system that had already been satisfactorily tested. The bombardment would come from the greatest force of artillery ever gathered in one place: over one million shells in just five hours, over three million during the first day. It would be big and multi-national; as a gesture of comradeship the artillery force would contain a small number of Austrian units – motorised heavy artillery.

Innovative in its design, the bombardment would be short and intense. There would be extensive use of lethal phosgene gas, against which the British gas masks provided protection, mixed with a new lachrymatory gas which the British gas masks could not handle. It was hoped that intense eye irritation would make the British remove their gas masks leaving them exposed to the toxic gas. Various combinations of gas and high explosive shells were to be used, the high explosive targeted on artillery emplacements, barbed wire, machine gun positions and trenches, and with an increased allotment of gas shells for the artillery sites.

Bruchmüller's plan contained a further innovation: the distance the bombardment would reach. To enable this, the artillery would be brought as close to the German front line as possible so that British back areas could be shelled in order to contain assembly areas and destroy unit headquarters. Although the preparations were thorough and the bombardment was to be very intense, the infantry knew that they would have to fight their way through the British positions; certainly the five-hour artillery attack would destroy artillery positions, wire and trenches but it would neither immobilise nor destroy the British infantry and machine gunners in their deeper dugouts.

Previous Western Front battles had been fought to a rigid timetable and with fixed objectives: with enough artillery on a single line of trenches, the attackers would take the position if their flank was secure. However, in a larger scale attack, the flank was often exposed or the attack foundered on the next set of trenches. For the 'Kaiserschlacht', the new ideas of Hauptmann Geyer would be employed: fluidity, infiltration and initiative; troops were to be given a direction of advance and told to proceed as rapidly as they could, ignoring their flanks. The *Sturmabteilungen* would spearhead the advance, ignoring strong points, and push through the weaker areas aided by a creeping artillery barrage, *das Feuerwalz* (the waltz of fire), timed to move forward 200 metres every four minutes; troops moving faster than this, could, by using rockets, have the barrage moved on more quickly. Apart from surprise and the new tactics, the German Army possessed one further advantage – 'the men were available to bring an almost overwhelming strength to bear on the line to be attacked.'

Although technically a secret, it was obvious to the soldiers concerned that an offensive was coming. Reliable divisions were taken out of the line, sent to back areas, re-equipped and trained for long periods of time, being replaced at the front by lower grade troops who normally held the quiet sectors. For the troops in training, food, for once, was reasonably abundant, rest in secure and reasonable conditions was possible, and there was time available for concerts, theatricals and lectures of a patriotic type. The luckiest were the artillery units, some of whom had to be sent back to Germany to re-equip. There was no doubt that manpower demands would be high, so, in order to provide further replacements, hospitals were emptied, and garrisons, orderly rooms and staff numbers were reduced to retain only essential men.

Of the sixty-three divisions available for the attack, only seven had not been through the special training programme and all were ready for the great offensive. They were prepared to enter the battle willingly, expecting success. Most realised that this was the battle that would settle the war one way or another; one soldier even wrote that in war-weary troops, as a result of the forthcoming attack, 'joy and euphoria made their appearance.' While many would fight to force the end, others had different reasons for wanting to get at the British – booty: 'the provisions, stores, cigarettes, tinned meat, biscuits. We knew what we were after.' wrote one soldier after the war. For most of the attacking troops, morale was high, but some were just glad of the break from the monotony of an existence in the trenches. For many it would be the first time that they had gone over the top, and, while the majority wondered whether they would survive, many were more concerned about not letting their comrades down.

The attack, code-named Operation Michael, was to fall on the British front. After considerable deliberation, Ludendorff decided upon the fifty-mile sector south of Arras down to La Fère because, after the winter, the ground would dry out quicker than in other British areas; also, very importantly, the British defences and forces were believed to be weak. After the initial onslaught, the troops would wheel right and move north, taking British positions in the rear. This was not to be one battle, but a whole series, to destroy the British army, or push it back to the sea. Just in case the French decided to help their allies, there were attacks scheduled against them.

The assault troops were brought up to the front on 20 March without serious difficulty, even though the British artillery shelled the front line trenches during the evening and night. For the men in the first wave, time passed slowly, and tension rose as zero hour approached. Then, at the appointed time, 4.40 am on 21 March, nearly 10,000 field guns and mortars opened fire on the British positions on a front between the Oise and Sensée rivers, shelling the area between the forward positions and the battle zone; four hours later the first wave of infantry charged out of the trenches and moved quickly towards the British lines through thick fog. Preceded by the *Sturmabteilungen*, forty-three divisions of *Second* and *Eighteenth* armies assaulted the British Fifth Army, while a further nineteen divisions of *Seventeenth* Army attacked the British Third Army. The well trained attackers were in excellent spirits and confident that they would win the war.

Outnumbered and hampered by the thick fog, the British forward zone of defence fell apart in many places. 'The infiltration tactics of the German infantry were eminently suited to the nature of the British defence, but were certainly favoured by the mistiness of the morning. The men of the advanced groups had rifles slung and made no attempt to use them, trusting the stick bombs with which they were well provided. When they reached a trench they hurled their bombs and at once jumped in to settle the defenders with club or bayonet. The next parties pushed on through the gaps and then came others to deal with the centres of resistance by means of machine guns, flame projectors, trench mortars and field guns.'

While all three armies made progress, in the south, against the weakest part of the British line, the *Eighteenth* Army had the most effect. Overall it was a day of limited success though, with less than a quarter of the first day's objectives achieved and with around 40,000 casualties. That it was not the success that had been hoped for is indicated by the brevity of the official communiqué on events: 'From south-east of Arras to La Fère we attacked the British positions. After a heavy bombardment of artillery and trench mortars our infantry assaulted on a wide front and everywhere captured the enemy's front lines.' In a similar vein, Admiral Müller, one of the Kaiser's chief advisors at Supreme Headquarters, recorded in his diary that 'the results of the offensive are not very satisfactory' and as a result the mood was low at breakfast next day.

The next day, further *Sturmabteilungen* and 'attack divisions' assaulted the British positions. Operation Michael continued, generally against stiffening resistance and British counterattacks, on one occasion with tanks, and with rising casualties, especially among officers who could only be replaced from divisions in the third line. Fortunately there was considerable confusion in the interpretation of the Orders issued by the senior British officers, and, as gaps appeared in the British lines, the German troops were quick to exploit them. By 24 March, the British had been pushed back, on average, fifteen miles, and had lost about 50,000 men as POWs.

The greatest success was enjoyed by *Eighteenth Army* that opened a serious gap in the British line. In less than a week, the most successful units were pushing forty miles into the British lines; but, although this was a significant distance, it was not in the area where breakthrough was really needed. The advance was moving southwest instead of northwest. It was also difficult to exploit the tactical success of the offensive as there was little cavalry available.

General Hutier's *Eighteenth Army*, originally intended to protect the left flank of the assault against any French attacks and to cover the advance of *Second Army*, had now 'become the spearhead from which even still greater successes were expected.' To the north, on *Second Army* front, the advance had been much slower, and apart from the centre, its objectives had not been reached; British counterattacks had slowed down the right flank but, in the south, even though the British rearguard fought determinedly, sometimes using cavalry and tanks, the German troops advanced to the Beaulencourt line by nightfall and made contact with *Seventeenth Army*. Little progress had been made by *Seventeenth Army* until the British Third Army pulled back. 'The resistance both north and south of the Scarpe, east of Arras, was very stiff, and there were counterattacks; in this sector only the *IX Reserve Corps* succeeded in breaking through at Henin and St. Martin, and at these places spirited charges of the British from Neuville Vitasse were repulsed.' One problem faced by the German troops in this sector was the old battlefield of the Somme that was covered by craters that made movement difficult; and as everything had been destroyed during the withdrawal a year previously there was little or no shelter to be had. In a letter home, one German soldier described the landscape they advanced through as 'a scene of terrible destruction. Crater after crater, some villages…have disappeared completely – a few splintered stumps is all that remain of the trees. The roads are littered with dead horses, corpses of Germans, Englishmen and Frenchmen, strewn with equipment, weapons, ammunition, here and there damaged English guns.' In the south the left flank was finding the going a little easier and Bapaume was captured after heavy fighting. As a result of this, the direction of attack for *Seventeenth Army* was changed towards Doullens instead of St. Pol in the north.

Provisioning the attackers before the offensive had been difficult. Only four days' supply of ammunition was available instead of the five days' originally planned; food was also short. One soldier wrote home complaining that there was bread but nothing to go with it, and reported that some soldiers were so hungry they would take 'any bacon or ham you might have that has gone mouldy.' What had not been possible before the start of the offensive was now proving to be even more difficult; there was insufficient horse-drawn or motorised transport to cross forty miles of devastated land successfully and there were not enough engineer troops to repair roads, lay new rail tracks and provide sufficient light railway stock. The further the army advanced, the more difficult it was for commanders to keep in touch with their men; this was due to a shortage of telephone wire - orders could take a day to reach their destination. Besides these internal logistic problems, there was always the British air force to contend with. British aircraft losses were greater than German ones, but the sheer number of British planes gave them overall air supremacy. As a result they were able to bomb and strafe military transport columns as they traversed the forward battle zones and also attack infantry positions and reinforcements.

Even though all had not gone to plan and there were considerable difficulties to overcome still, the Kaiser was overjoyed by what he thought was a victory and ordered the flags to be flown and a victory salute to be fired to celebrate his army's triumphs at Cambrai, Monchy, La Fère and St. Quentin on 25 March. As a reward for the success of the offensive, he awarded Hindenburg the Iron Cross with Golden Rays (the last recipient of the award had been Field Marshal Blücher in 1814) and Ludendorff the Grand Cross of the Iron Cross. Many officers quietly felt that the Kaiser was being overly optimistic.

Stubbornly the British and Empire troops failed to realise that they should have been beaten. To the south, fierce resistance by the French further slowed down the advance and, on 27 March, an attack on British positions near Rosières was met by such strong opposition that casualties were roughly equal on both sides – but among the German losses were many of the irreplaceable *Sturmabteilungen* troops. It appeared that the British had learned and applied the lessons of the last week.

Operation Mars was launched the next day; it aimed to trap the northern British armies by attacking northwest from Arras, and was to prepare the way for a breakout towards the channel ports. However, unlike 21 March, there was no fog to hide behind and the British knew what to expect. In addition the attack had been planned hurriedly. After three hours' bombardment, the attack was launched at 7.30 am on 28 March. Unfortunately for the German attackers, casualties were very heavy for little territorial gain.

The offensive continued, but huge losses, exhaustion and the lack of a decisive breakthrough, linked with an ever increasing length of supply chain and a shortage of supplies, even food, were taking their toll on morale. Low spirits and incidents of disobedience and drunkenness when British supply dumps and French towns were overrun were the result. Binding recorded in his post-war memoirs what he had seen in Albert after *3 Marine Division* had looted the town: 'Men driving cows before them on a line; others who carried a hen under one arm and a box of notepaper under the other. Men carrying a bottle of wine under their arm and another one open in their hand – men dressed up in comic disguise. Men with top-hats on their heads. Men staggering. Men who could hardly walk at all.' Accusations about divisions not pursuing the British troops because of drunkenness were later shown to be untrue. It was the determination of the British defences that was the key issue in checking the advance.

After months of shortages and falling quality of goods and material, the German troops were amazed to see how well provisioned the British troops were – a direct contradiction to the propaganda that the submarine attacks were starving Britain. A commander of a squadron of Dragoons wrote after the war that they 'were greatly impressed by the British Army's equipment and marvelled at their leather jerkins, their puttees and their excellent boots', and in no time they were making the most of the captured booty: 'smoking highly prized Virginia cigarettes, polishing their boots with shoe polish and riding around in cars with rubber tyres'. Luxuries like these 'were unheard-of things which belong to a fairyland of long ago.'

On a military basis, a German writer poetically summed up the Mars attack: 'As the sun set behind rain clouds there also vanished the hopes which O.H.L. had placed on the attack. "Mars", to whom so much blood was offered, was unable to break open the British Arras salient.' At midnight on 28 March, the Mars offensive was cancelled but the general attacks continued along the front with minor success. Apart from the determined resistance of the British defenders, a further factor was playing its part on the German side – hunger; only so much could be expected of troops who had been in action continuously for sixty-plus hours and had not eaten for forty-eight, except stocks available for plunder. There was a shortage of reinforcements so divisions had to be kept at the front to keep up the momentum. The troops were getting both physically and mentally tired. Some fought for eight days without taking off their boots or clothes, though this mattered less as the only water for washing was that in the shell holes. Even drinking water was in short supply.

'The final result of the day is the unpleasant fact that our offensive has come to a complete stop'. Ludendorff later wrote that 'the enemy's resistance was beyond our powers'. Operation Michael was suspended on 5 April, with the Germans finding themselves in defensive positions on the muddy Somme battlefield that they had voluntarily left a year earlier. Although the assault had cost them more casualties than they had inflicted, they had captured 90,000 Allied soldiers and 1,300 artillery pieces. In terms of distance, *Second Army* had advanced forty-five kilometres and *Eighteenth Army* up to sixty kilometres. However, the success had created its own problems in terms of supply. There was now a very large salient vulnerable to counterattack in certain places; the plans now being adopted were tactical rather than strategic; the casualties could not be replaced in either number or quality. The British on the other hand had over 100,000 trained soldiers ready for use in France before the end of the month, the French army had lost little of its fighting strength and was now recovered from its problems of May 1917, and there were thousands of Americans arriving on a weekly basis. The French Army intelligence service had also noted the deteriorating quality of the German front line soldier since 21 March.

Before the next full-scale offensive, Ludendorff planned a diversionary attack against the French in the Aisne sector, to seize the high ground to the east of the Oise-Aisne canal in order to improve the position of *Eighteenth Army*. Due to a lack of horses and troops, this was postponed from 31 March until 6 April. It followed the previous pattern of a gas barrage at 03.30 hrs on the French artillery positions, followed at 4.25am when over 200 batteries shelled the French positions; sixty-five minutes later, the *Sturmabteilungen* attacked, meeting very little resistance. As a result of this success, General von Boehn ordered the advance to continue the next day to establish bridgeheads across the canal. Heavy overnight rain and stiffer resistance slowed down the advance, but all objectives were taken and the next day the attack continued. During the night of 8 April, the French troops pulled back to the west bank of the canal,

A soldier in drag enjoys the attentions of one of his comrades during a rest period.

An artillery repair workshop – all available guns would be needed in March and each had to be in excellent condition for accurate firing.

leaving the Germans to take the east bank without opposition. Further diversionary attacks were made to establish bridgeheads on the west bank, but all available troops were placed at the disposal of the Crown Prince's Army Group.

The purpose of this attack was to disguise preparations for the real offensive to the north – Operation Georgette, which, due to the high casualty rate of Operation Michael was a scaled-down version of the original Operation Saint George. It was to be launched on Ludendorff's 53rd birthday, 9 April, against Hazebrouck, with the intention of cutting off the BEF from its supply routes. But, true to the previous year and the British attacks on the Arras front, launching an offensive on such a date was not a wise choice.

Although the plan was apparently sound, the defending British defences in this sector were stronger than those attacked on 21 March. Moreover, many of the attacking units were not top quality troops and, in many cases, they had been only hastily trained; fortunately for the German troops the British did not have the luxury of a large number of reserves to combat any attack and, again, luckily for the Germans, the assault was made in a thick fog.

The artillery barrage for Georgette started at 04.15 hrs. Due to the lack of wind, the gas shells were very effective. A heavy mist covered the battlefield, allowing the troops to move up to the front with little interference from British guns. Initially the progress of the attack was excellent; by the end of the first day the assault had moved forward three and a half miles and pushed through the already demoralised 2 Portuguese Division which, after offering only feeble resistance, either ran or surrendered, leaving the bridges intact for a more rapid German advance. But the going was not as easy in other parts of the line, especially on the extreme south of the attack, where one British division put up a very strong defence. In spite of repeated attacks and considerable casualties, by the end of the day no real progress had been made in this sector. Along with the heavy toll of dead and wounded, over 600 troops, including two battalion commanders, and a band (with its musical instruments) were taken prisoner when they were caught in the British wire and had no choice but to surrender; also captured were more than a hundred machine guns and automatic weapons. Crown Prince Rupprecht noted that this failure was due to the obstinate resistance of a particularly good Scottish division; in reality the British troops were from Lancashire and would probably have been extremely insulted if they had known!

The fog had proved to be useful, but the general weather conditions were, in fact, more of a hindrance to the attacking German troops. Rainy weather immediately before 'had hampered air reconnaissance, made road building impossible, and had a disastrous effect on morale'. As a result of the rain, everything slowed down; the mud that was so deep that fascines and planks sank into it, with the result that supplies had to be dropped from the air.

The next day, von Arnim's *Fourth Army* assaulted Messines Ridge at 05.15 hrs, after a two and a half hour bombardment, through dense mist over previously-laid pontoon bridges across the River Lys. Messines and part of the ridge fell to *17 Reserve Division*, but stiffening British resistance slowed down the advance that eventually formed a defensive line between Hill 63 and the southern end of Messines across the Douve valley. Further south, Ploegsteert village was taken and held against fierce British counterattacks, but little progress was made into Ploegsteert Wood.

Although at 06.00 hrs *Sixth Army* resumed its attack, it continued to make little progress against fierce resistance. With reinforcements arriving the next day, they were ordered to take the high ground around Bailleul and Meteren on the Franco-Belgian border and the crossings over La Bassée canal. A major success during the day was the British evacuation of Armentières and, by the next day, *Sixth Army* was only five miles away from Hazebrouck. However, fresh British and Empire units were arriving just as Georgette was beginning to 'run out of steam' because the troops were exhausted and disillusioned. Changes in the command structure of the British and French forces also resulted in the arrival of French divisions in the British sector. Later the British withdrawal from Passchendaele frustrated the German attacks on Ypres and, by the end of the month, the offensive was beginning to look like a failure, especially when Hazebrouck was not captured.

On 11 April, the Kaiser arrived at *Fourth Army* Headquarters. During his visit he sent a message to the troops that was conveyed to them by the Army Commander; 'the Kaiser expressed his best wishes and thanks for the efforts made hitherto, also his firm conviction that in the coming days each individual would do all he could to ensure a decisive victory over our British enemy'.

While *Sixth Army* made better progress on 12 April with an advance of up to six kilometres, its troops had received little in the way of food rations as it was impossible to get the field kitchens through the mud. The troops found much to eat in the deserted British trenches and the advance slowed down as they ate their fill. There were also some severe disciplinary problems reported. As the Germans slowed down, the British intensified their defence with strong counterattacks, succeeding in pushing the Germans back. There were also 'serious transport difficulties owing to artillery fire, bombing, and congestion on the few roads available; the regimental transport consisted of anything from a landau to a hand-barrow, and the condition of the horses was dreadful'. The difficulties and conditions are described in the history of *12 Reserve Field Artillery Regiment (12 Reserve Division)*: 'The march was carried out under extreme difficulties, owing to entire lack of road control and hour-long blocks on the road' and even though engineers tried to put bridges over the trenches and mend the roads, 'it was most troublesome to get forward. There were everywhere signs of fighting. The flight of the Portuguese had evidently been exceptionally rapid' because in the cottages along the road 'foodstuff was still on the table, and in the field were scattered guns with the shells still in the bore.' When they reached Estaires it was still burning and the roads in and out of the town were blocked with troops 'offering splendid targets to the enemy airmen. The infantry, as well as the artillery, suffered very heavy losses in the afternoon and during the night', with one regiment losing sixty men while marching through Estaires. Eventually the regiment stopped to rest 'but the very welcome short rest was broken by enemy airmen, who searched the ground and threw bombs.'

On 13 April, heavy losses were incurred from British artillery that had been brought forward to well-concealed positions with excellent observation, and the attack on Bailleul failed, due to machine gun and rifle fire as the Germans slowly moved forward through the mud. The crack Bavarian Alpine troops, however, did manage to get within twenty-five yards of the British front line where they were stopped. These troops were held responsible for the failure and replaced by *III Bavarian Corps*. After the war an officer of the *Alpine Corps* recorded that having fought in Italy, Serbia, Rumania and at Verdun he felt that 'the defenders on the British front in April 1918 were the best troops of the many with whom we crossed swords in the course of the four and a quarter years.'

The next day little progress was made and in some places ground was lost to British counterattacks, but Ludendorff, who had become arrogant and inflexible, wanted the offensive to continue – against the wishes of many of the Corps Commanders. They wanted time to take stock and replace ammunition and supplies and to rest the exhausted men. Some units were mutinous and were refusing to fight even when directly ordered. However, on *Fourth Army* front, troops advanced two kilometres and took Bailleul on 15 April. Further south, *Sixth Army* made limited gains and also took the high ground at Meteren and Wytschaete the next day, even beating off the strong British counterattacks. Crown Prince Rupprecht echoed the comments about the difficulty faced in moving forward in the area: 'Everywhere I heard complaints about the difficulty of finding shelter for man and beast in the completely devastated area, and about the heavy losses caused by bombing attacks, especially in horses, which had no protection even from view in their lines.'

Convinced that the British would not defend Mont Kemmel, a surprise attack was planned for 18 April, along with further attacks at Festubert and Givenchy. These last were almost successful, but the first assault was destroyed by a carefully placed British artillery barrage. One attacking division, *6 Bavarian*, was shown to have no fighting strength left after having been badly mauled the day before and after careful consideration further attacks in the area were postponed.

The situation changed further when it was noted that the French were preparing a major attack between Montdidier and Noyon and around Moreuil. On 18 April, a strong French attack was beaten off, but the French took the high ground to the west of Castel, providing them with clear observation of the German positions in the Avre and Luce valleys.

A 'Happy New Year'? – troops in transit to the Western front.

Heavy artillery quartered near Bethancourt waiting to be moved to the front.

Taken in the summer of 1917, a well stocked and dug-in field gun. Artillery like this would have to follow the advancing troops to provide them with protection.

By now the German troops were utterly exhausted. It became clear to OHL that there was now no chance of taking Amiens. There were also signs of a breakdown in discipline: officers were losing authority, evident in the looting, vandalism and drunkenness that was reported. Exhaustion left the German troops unable to perform their duties; they could not advance, shoot their rifles or get out of the way of British fire. Fortunately many of the British units were equally exhausted.

Further attacks followed, and, by 24 April, German troops further south had reached Villers-Bretonneux, the site of a failed assault between 4 and 5 April. The original start date had already been put back until 23 April, when British bombers destroyed the railway line between Chaulnes and Guillaucourt by exploding 50,000 rounds of ammunition, causing huge logistical problems. It was during the preparations for this battle that the air ace, Baron von Richthofen, was killed on a reconnaissance flight.

As with previous attacks, there was a two and a half hour preliminary barrage with the infantry leaving their positions at 07.15 hrs in thick fog. After heavy fighting *4 Guards Division* took Villers-Bretonneux and continued on to the woods to reach their first day's objective. The left flank was less successful and fell back in panic after a British counterattack at 21.00 hrs. A hastily prepared British counterattack in the early hours of 25 April, with two Australian and one British brigade, was not held, and a further attack by a British division pushed the German troops out of Hangard Wood. By the end of the morning, the British had retaken the village, forcing the entire German front onto the defensive. Seven fresh British and French divisions had faced ten tired German divisions of poor fighting spirit who had not resisted the counterattacks and in some cases panicked. Further loss of morale was caused by reserves not being brought up quickly enough.

During the attack on 24 April, a German A7V tank approached the British lines that were partially protected by three British tanks, two 'females' armed only with machine guns and one 'male' with two six-pounder naval guns; the first tank-to-tank combat occurred when all four tanks went into action. The two machine gun tanks were soon hit and had to retire, but the remaining British tank eventually hit the A7V, forcing it to retire.

The final throw of Operation Georgette happened the next day with the assault of Mont Kemmel. From 03.30 hrs, gas shells rained down on British artillery positions and at 6am the hill was bombarded with high explosives, much of which landed in the tightly-packed trenches of the French 28 Division. One hour later, the infantry began the assault with the elite *Alpine Corps* attacking the French positions head on. Within seventy minutes they had reached the summit and, thirty minutes later, reported that it was in their possession. *56 Division* took Kemmel village. General von Lossberg wanted to continue the offensive but Ludendorff told him to wait for the artillery to be brought up so the German troops dug in and waited. By the end of the day, the offensive was called off with little gain except over 2,000 British POWs, four artillery pieces and a small amount of territory – this at the cost of about 8,000 casualties.

Reliable intelligence from aerial reconnaissance and deciphered British radio-traffic was corroborated by the statements of French POWs – there would be a large scale Allied counteroffensive in the near future. On the morning of 26 April, just as they were preparing to continue their own offensive, they were attacked by three Allied divisions after a heavy artillery barrage. Although it was held, it meant that the German attack could not start until the afternoon. By then, the troops were tired and the artillery short of shells; little progress was made and General Arnim von Sixt ordered a temporary break in offensive operations until 29 April.

To the north, they were hoping to remove the British from the Ypres salient. On 29 April they made a seven division attack, with six divisions in reserve. 'The artillery bombardment was to open with gas shelling, which was to last as long as the supplies with the batteries allowed, but not beyond 05.00 hrs' and 'for the next forty minutes, hurricane fire was to be poured on the hostile positions'. There was considerable complaint about the supply of ammunition, and, up to the afternoon of 28 April, *4 Bavarian Division* had received no gas shells. At 05.40 hrs the first wave rose to advance after the two-and-a-half hour artillery barrage assisted by aircraft. However, prisoner interrogations had alerted the British and the assaulting infantry faced ten British divisions. By 08.00 hrs it was obvious the attack was in difficulty; at 10.45

hrs Hindenburg debated whether to call the attack off; at 12 noon General von Lossberg reported solid resistance and high casualties from artillery and machine guns. In response to an enquiry from the Kaiser, General von Lossberg, Chief of Staff of *Fourth Army* informed him that although there had been considerable difficulty the action would be continued later in the day with three units; *233 Division* attacked but made no progress, the Alpine Corps did not bother to attack at all, and *4 Bavarian Division* was simply too exhausted to make any further efforts that day. At 22.20 hrs that night the attack was cancelled but commanding officers were given permission to undertake minor operations if they wanted to. 'The whole Georgette operation was finished; the *Fourth* and *Sixth Armies* had exhausted their powers of attack. No great strategic movement had become possible'. Neither had the Channel ports been reached.

Although much territory had been captured since 21 March, OHL acknowledged that the three offensives had not destroyed the British as had been intended, and that overall they had failed because their objectives had been too ambitious. Casualties had been equally high on both sides, but the enemy could rely upon large numbers of American troops replacing any losses; this was not the case for the German Army. Not only could the German losses not be easily replaced in number, but they could never be replaced in quality as the best troops had been allocated to the *Sturmabteilungen* and the assault divisions where the losses were greatest. Kitchen sums up the situation: 'the British had suffered 25,000 casualties since 21 March. Twelve of their sixty-two divisions were mere skeletons, and the two Portuguese divisions were out of action for the foreseeable future.' The other major member of the Entente, the French, 'had lost about 100,000 men, and forty-three of their 103 infantry divisions had been involved in the fighting, along with six cavalry divisions.' The Americans were arriving in ever increasing numbers, but at that time there were only four fully formed divisions over which there had been disputes concerning how they would be used when ready. Because of a lack of shipping, the flow of trained soldiers was not at the target level. And, as for the Germans, with 206 divisions they 'still had a considerable advantage' but 'they were tired and desperately short of recruits. They had lost more men in April than they had in March, and there was a noticeable decline in fighting spirit. Their artillery and airforce were worn down by constantly being moved from one battlefield to another, and both arms were inferior to those of the Entente.' The decline in morale among the fighting men had reached some of the senior commanders who realised that they would have to go back onto the defensive and that the war could not be won with further offensives.

While some senior officers cautioned an end to the offensives, Ludendorff disagreed. He did however accept that there was no longer the ability to fight two offensives at the same time. Instead of destroying the British forces, he decided to turn against the French in a series of smaller attacks that would separate them from the British.

The High Command had learned lessons from the three previous offensives. It had changed the role of the artillery, modified tactics to deal with the French method of defence and the terrain, and had provided specialist training for the fresh troops who were incorporated into the assault divisions. Much emphasis had been placed on training for the attack in waves and in small groups (to reduce the size of the target they offered to the enemy defenders) and in the use of their weapons in the attack, particularly the light machine guns. Although there were complaints about the new tactics, they were effective in reducing casualties in later attacks. Further training was given to allay the myth of tank supremacy; men were shown how to disable tanks with grenades, mortars, high powered rifles, and artillery firing over open sites.

Two further offensives were being prepared by *Seventh Army* – Blücher (named for the Field Marshall who helped defeat Napoleon) and Goerz (a swashbuckling sixteenth-century mercenary famed for his comment – 'Lick my arse!') by *First Army*. The Blücher offensive against the defences on the Ailette and Oise-Aisne canal crossed a marshy battlefield of water-filled shell craters; the Chemin des Dames offered the French an excellent view of the German deployment for the battle – not surprisingly, the French positions were only lightly manned. In one attempt the Germans had to advance eighteen kilometres over difficult terrain including two canals, two ridges and a river before reaching their target, Fismes on the River

Vesle. The conditions for Operation Goerz were similarly very difficult – crossing the Aisne-Marne canal, fighting uphill in wooded countryside, then bridging the River Aisne – thirty-five metres wide at the point of attack – and assaulting French positions in place since 1914.

Each of the two offensive fronts had only eight divisions apiece instead of the required total of thirty-six divisions; only eight of the divisions would be fresh. At the end of April, the picture was bleak. Each of the assault battalions needed to be equipped and trained and most of the battalions were short of up to 200 men. A further problem was the morale of the reinforcements from the Eastern Front, of whom round about twenty percent deserted, being rewarded with four months in prison.

German deception did not provide the French with sufficient clues about where the attack would fall, only that it would fall, perhaps in the Champagne region or Lorraine or on the Chemin des Dames, Reims, Nancy or Verdun. However, the British thought that the brunt would fall on them near Arras. This was achieved by leaving thirty assault divisions opposite them in Flanders and in the Somme area. To further deceive the British, extra bivouac fires were lit, 'large numbers of troops were marched about, telephones, wireless and visual signalling were kept busy and many air attacks against the rear areas were made in order to distract attention from the Aisne front.'

Security precautions in the attack area were very strict and followed those of the previous offensives, with only those needing to know having access to the plans and with strict orders to conceal every aspect of the build-up for the offensive. Even the divisions in position were to be misled with the information that a few tired divisions were to be replaced and the artillery were only allowed one round to register their potential targets. In order to allow good communication during the attack, around 2,500 miles of telephone cable were laid, mostly for artillery use, while attacking troops in the first wave were to rely upon hand-carried wireless equipment. In order to allow communication across the Ailette river, submarine cable was to be provided.

The number of artillery batteries and the amount of ammunition needed was a serious problem with the first batteries arriving on 14 May, and the last on 23 May. The mass of batteries were in position before daylight on 26 May to allow the infantry to move forward freely. Lacking concealment, batteries were hidden wherever, to be man-handled into position on the night of 25/26 May, with the last few being brought up during the night of 26/27 May. The next problem was to deliver and conceal six days' supply of ammunition (approximately 320,000 shells of all calibres) which was not achieved until the night of 26 May: 'the bringing up of trench-mortar ammunition…close to the front line gave even greater trouble.' A further problem that had to be surmounted was that of the bridges and roads. Moving the infantry into place at a safe distance behind the lines proved comparatively simple.

The French Army staff eventually realised that there was a threat to the Chemin des Dames. Seven divisions were brought up to bolster the defences, and, when German prisoners taken in raids gave appropriate information, General Duchêne moved his reserves into the battle zone. During the night of 26 and 27 May, German positions were shelled causing some casualties, but this barrage did not stop the troops moving into the forward positions.

On 27 May, at 01.00 hrs, 4000 guns began a two-hour-and-forty-minute barrage on the French positions, at a concentration higher than 21 March. Contrary to Allied doctrine, these positions were packed with troops and not thinly held. Seventeen assault divisions launched themselves, through a light mist, at the stunned French troops at exactly 03.40 hrs. Within hours the attackers had forced a gap between the British and French defenders and by 05.30 hrs they had reached the Chemin des Dames. Five of the divisions making up the French forces were recuperating from the previous offensives and, ironically, three of them were in the front line when the attack came and these offered little resistance. With the defenders caught completely off guard, they rapidly pushed forward to cross the River Aisne and had reached the River Vesle by evening: an advance of up to twelve miles that included the capture of bridges and an airfield with fuel and aircraft.

Not every division was prepared to put in the full effort and, as in previous offensives, there were problems with discipline. Two divisions in particular were singled out as lacking fighting spirit – 7 *Reserve* and *86 Division*. Both divisions made only slight progress in their attack on one British division during 28 May. 'The infantry of the *7th Reserve Division* was greatly lacking in attack ardour on this day' noted the official history and an artillery commander reported that they 'stopped in the face of weak resistance, went forward very slowly with hour-long pauses, without there being any question of any real fighting.' Later on the same day the division found a deserted supply dump and 'there were regrettable excesses – one saw melancholy sights and cases of serious drunkenness.' The *Official History* recorded an even more lack-lustre attack by *86 Division* that 'went forward even more slowly than the *7th Reserve* and, going no further than Thil-Trigny, lost all touch with the Allies.' A third unit, *232 Division*, also failed in its attack. Like *86 Division*, it was from the Russian Front and this was the reason given for their failure, while *7 Reserve, 52* and *103 Divisions* were deemed to have failed because they were not doing their duty.

Soissons was captured the next day and by 3 June the leading divisions had reached the River Marne and were only about fifty miles from Paris; from this distance Big Bertha could once again menace Paris. But tiredness and a shortage of men and ammunition, plus increasing French resistance from fresh troops, was slowing the attack down. French air power was also having an effect on troop movements and bombing attacks were destroying much-needed supplies. The advance on 4 June was modest while the next day, at considerable loss, minor positional changes were made by *7 Army*.

Operation Blücher was an unqualified success – but the Americans were waiting, and, on 6 June, they cut the German offensive at Belleau Wood. The next problem to be faced was maintaining the newly created salient so Operation Blücher was called off, to be replaced by Operation Gneisenau; this was an attack against the French between Montdidier and Noyon. But now troop losses were increasing from a new enemy – Spanish influenza, which previously had mainly affected the enemy. On 9 June, the infantry of *Eighteenth Army*, after a three hour twenty-five minute artillery barrage, assaulted the French Third Army at 04.20 hrs through thick fog, their own gas and across difficult terrain, on a twenty-one mile front. They made a six-mile advance capturing 8,000 French POWs but, unlike Blücher, the advance slowed down quickly and on 11 June was halted completely, due to strong French counterattacks which included artillery support, tanks and low-flying aircraft strafing the advancing German troops.

The attack by *First Army* was poorly prepared, short of ammunition and reliant on tired men; initial success turned into a retreat to the start line in the face of heavy artillery fire and skilful counterattacks. Neither Blücher nor Gneisenau had delivered the much-needed breakthrough, although the German troops had advanced as far as ten miles, taken 15,000 POWs and 300 guns. The French forces suffered a total of 40,000 casualties against German casualties of 25,000. Once again the German army had lost the best of its men, but, for the Allies, the Americans kept coming. Similarly, lost guns could easily be replaced by the Allies. The German forces could replace neither men nor materiel. The battle was scheduled to continue, but French artillery bombardments and counterattacks made it impossible for the Germans to achieve the targets set for Operation Hammer Blow, and, where attempted, they failed. Continuing French counterattacks forced a decision. Operation Gneiseau was stopped and Operation Hammer Blow was to be cancelled after just two days.

Preparations for a further advance along the Aisne continued with Operation Hammer Blow. It began at 05.00 hrs on 12 June, after a ninety-minute barrage. The Allied forces had moved their artillery back out of range so the German barrage did not affect its ability to return fire. The result was heavy German losses, with only the left flank reaching its objectives two kilometres from the starting line; continued fighting the next day produced nothing except casualties and adjustments to the line, so, on 14 June the attacks were cancelled.

As with previous assaults, much booty was captured and there were incidents of drunken orgies. As a result, discipline collapsed, generally in the rear. The draw of booty was a contributing factor in moving the offensive forward, but had the downside that the advance was interrupted while the troops gorged on what they took. Later, each division had a Spoils Officer and each regiment a Spoils Troop; reliable men, responsible for handing out captured alcohol, clothing, food and tobacco for immediate consumption, and who handed over the remainder to the Military Police for distribution to the rear echelons; a certain

A base hospital well behind the lines complete with two red crosses to discourage enemy aircraft.

Officers of *142 Infantry Regiment* near a guard point. Manpower was to be a significant factor in the coming assaults so much so that men with one arm could still be in the army – note the officer in the centre with the Blue Max around his neck.

A false gun position complete with fake gun to trick Allied photographic interpreters.

amount was kept in reserve for later. Not all units were lucky enough to capture enough booty to satisfy their needs. Some soldiers were reduced to eating the flesh of horses killed by enemy action. Later, a special bonus was paid for another spoil of war, enemy equipment and weapons.

A decision now had to made about the best way forward; there were two options, Operation Hagen and Operation Roland; it was decided that first option was the better one. Ludendorff gave his approval and Hagen was scheduled for the end of July. Many senior officers realised that it could not be decisive, as Ludendorff hoped, because of the manpower shortage. With the amount of artillery and troop movement needed, as well as reinforcements to bring divisions up to strength, it became apparent that Hagen would be unable to start on the planned date and by mid-June it was apparent that Hagen was highly unlikely to happen.

Ludendorff had failed to provide the breakthrough that would end the war and, both at home and among many of the troops, there was a feeling of inevitability about the future; further attacks that would have initial gains but no breakthrough, allied counterattacks and all the time the butcher's bill was getting bigger. On the home front physical lethargy was breeding mental despair. There were two overriding needs - food and peace. By May, food had become so scarce that, according to Princess Blücher, even the kangaroos in Berlin Zoo were slaughtered for their meat. In June, Berliners were limited to one pound of potatoes – often rotten - a week. Initially the food shortage had affected only the adults, who had been able to ensure that their children had enough food. Food was now so scarce in the towns that the children were as 'thin and pale as corpses', as one doctor recorded. But it was not just food that was in short supply: everything that was needed for everyday living was either unavailable, existed as an ersatz product or was so expensive only the rich could afford it. There was mounting resentment against the war profiteer and the black marketeer, both groups clearly evidence of a divided society. This inevitably led to a breakdown of discipline and order and an increase in violent crime and theft, particularly of food.

At home there had been random acts of sabotage and strikes that had badly affected military production and jeopardised the planned offensives. Even the victories did not alter the public feeling and, by May, with the offensive taking the troops to the Marne, the mood was one of apathy. Socialist and pacifist propaganda was also having its effect upon the people's hopes and aspirations. People declared themselves 'tired of suffering'. What they wanted was the return of their sons and husbands.

The Russian Revolution had left its mark on many soldiers who had been on the Eastern Front. Coupled with the discontent at home which percolated to the men at the front, the pacifist and socialist propaganda was beginning to have a serious effect. It was reported that a train bringing replacements for 2 Bavarian Division had 'Red Guards' painted on the carriages' and that infractions of military discipline were becoming more common. Rupprecht's diary contains a comment that confirms this problem: he noted the 'mutinous resistance of reinforcements being sent to the front' while Ludendorff, in his memoirs, recorded that there had been 'a decided deterioration in the Army's morale resulting from the re-enrolment, after long leave, of soldiers returned from captivity in Russia; they introduced a spirit of general insubordination.' Ludendorff and Rupprecht thought that the causes of declining morale were war-weariness, the failure of the supply system, influenza, units being under-strength and reinforcements of indifferent morale. As well as a falling-off in the troops' ability to resist Allied attacks as ably as they had done in previous months, the British also noticed that their opponents 'had ceased to trouble about burying or removing the dead, or to make latrines.' The shortage of reinforcements, according to Ludendorff, was causing the greatest anxiety' and 'one division (9 Bavarian) had been broken up' to provide reinforcements, while others would also have to be disbanded.

Two further attacks were ordered on 14 June as a precondition for Operation Hagen. The plans for Operation Marne were to be drawn up by Seventh Army and the plans for Operation Reims by First Army. To be effective they would have to take place before the Americans really did arrive in force because of the manpower shortage in the German Army. Even the rigid combing out of every male who was not essentially employed in the war industries failed to provide enough men; future attacks would use lightly-wounded men and troops from the back areas who could be replaced by older and less physically-fit men, including one-armed men doing jobs where only one arm was needed. Losses at the front were running at around 1,000 men every day and there was inadequate artillery for two simultaneous offensives. Hagen was therefore postponed until the end of July – but, if it went ahead, there would not be enough divisions for Operation Reims. While the German commanders were trying to decide their best move, the British attacked Albert, Béthune and Moreuil, and further attacks north and south of the Somme succeeded in taking the high ground near Hamel. There was also evidence that they were preparing to attack the *Fourth* and *Sixth Armies* to slow down preparations for operations near Reims.

A further German manpower crisis was resulting from Spanish flu – *Sixth Army* reported that 15,000 men had caught the illness. The shortage of men was so desperate that Ludendorff had arranged for *1* and *15 Austrian Divisions* to be sent to the Western Front in July and more were to follow in September. The war in the east was officially over but garrison duties and continued Russian resistance against further German penetration tied down over forty infantry divisions that were needed on the Western Front; one division was transferred in June and broken up to provide reinforcements, and a further nine divisions were sent during September and October.

General directive number four from General Foch, to Generals Haig and Pétain, on 1 July, although it was on the subject of future operations, described how successful the German attacks had been over the past few months. 'Today, 1st July, the enemy has halted: 18 miles from Dunkirk, 36 miles from Calais, 42 miles from Boulogne, 36 miles from Abbeville, 36 miles from Paris, 15 miles from Châlons.' Of these, he deduced that Abbeville and Paris were the two most important areas to deal with. 'An advance of 24 miles towards Abbeville would cut the communications with the north of France, and separate the British and French Armies – a result of considerable military importance for the issue of the war.' 'An even smaller advance towards Paris', while not as strategically important in a military sense, 'would make a profound impression on public opinion, cause the evacuation of the capital under the menace of bombardment' and hamper the free action of the government.

Fortunately for the Allies, although an offensive was to be prepared, these were not to be the immediate areas for the next German attack. This planned offensive - Operation Kurfürst (Elector) – was to be towards both Paris and Amiens at the same time using two Army Groups. However, when it was realised that the resources were available, OHL stated that they would decide upon which of the two thrusts would take place only after Reims and Hagen; Kurfürst would begin no earlier than the middle of September. On 11 July, Hagen was postponed until 1 August, but its launch was now dependent upon the success of Operation Reims. Taking troops from *Eighteenth Army* to strengthen the attacks around Reims left the front lines sparsely manned, allowing the French to break through on a two-to-three kilometre front to a depth of up to one kilometre, while taking large numbers of prisoners and machine guns.

Confident of success, Ludendorff believed that success on 15 July would improve home front morale and bring the French to their knees. However, there were concerns: replacements for casualties would be a real problem, some of the chosen attack terrain would be very difficult to cross, most divisions had been hit by influenza that reduced the effective number of soldiers considerably, and the quality of the infantry was declining. A problem the OHL did not know about was that the French were aware of what was going to happen. Rumours of the offensive were confirmed by German POWs of *228 Division* and corroborated by escaped French POWs. The attack area, between Château-Thierry and Reims, was confirmed by a captured German aviator and when, towards the end of June, the French *Deuxième Bureau* (Secret Intelligence) found out that all leave had been cancelled in the German armies involved in the attack, and reconnaissance observed large numbers of ammunition trucks moving about, it was obvious that the offensive was about to start. The date and time were later given to the French by captured German soldiers. In response to this intelligence, French artillery opened up on 100 kilometres of the Reims front for a short while. The German artillery replied at 01.10 hrs.

On 15 July, French positions near Reims were bombarded by over 5,000 artillery pieces in the Reims-Marne Schutz or Second Battle of the Marne and at 04.50 hrs forty-three divisions assaulted the thinly-held French observation line. Unfortunately the opposing French Fourth Army was well aware of the plan

New soldiers called up at the start of 1918 who would soon find themselves on the Western Front – their mixed age suggests a combination of 18 year olds and men from previously reserved occupations.

A war cemetery. The coming offensives would see the construction of many more of these.

A field hospital in Flanders, June 1918. The lorry is pulling four wagons for transporting the wounded.

and, when they did attack, the survivors were caught by artillery and machine guns. However, *Seventh Army* made good progress and crossed the Marne with only light casualties before meeting stiffer resistance to the south of the river, and to the north broke through the main line of defence, even though the Italian defenders fought fiercely to hold their positions. To the east of Reims *First Army* made good progress and took the front line positions but a further advance was halted by exceptionally strong defensive positions. *Third Army* on the left flank made excellent initial progress but, like *First Army,* were halted at the main French line of defence. Although the offensive was only a limited success, it was decided to continue it the next day but with reduced goals – merely encircling Reims; this would allow two divisions to be sent to Army Gruppe Crown Prince Rupprecht for use in Operation Hagen.

A counterattack by the American 3 Division successfully pushed the Germans back to the main line of resistance and in some places beyond, and in the evening of 15 July the French launched a series of counterattacks preceded by a massive artillery barrage and supported with tanks. The ferocious French attacks were beaten back, but the cost was so high that it was not possible to continue the offensive the next day. On 17 July, OHL gave permission for the troops south of the Marne to retire to the north bank because of supply difficulties caused by a shortage of intact bridges.

The offensive had been stopped and Hagen was now likely to be cancelled; the final offensive had failed and as if to confirm the situation *Third Army* issued defensive orders on the same day. There was to be no retirement unless ordered by army headquarters and the first and second lines of defence were to be held at all costs. However, Ludendorff still wanted to go ahead with Hagen and numbers of troops were sent to Flanders; he also moved his headquarters to Tournai to prepare for the new offensive. On 18 July, during a meeting at which Ludendorff was dismissing the possibility of a French attack, news arrived that the French had attacked in force, south-west of Soissons with large numbers of tanks, catching the defenders by surprise; in order to contain the breakthrough it was necessary to send there some of the troops earmarked for Hagen. Continued French attacks, although eventually held, resulted in considerable loss of territory and brought essential railway lines under French artillery fire.

The High Command now felt confident that although they had halted the French attacks at great cost, the enemy had also suffered greatly and were no longer in a position to continue their offensive. However, on 22 July there were further attacks and more ground was lost. The army was now on the defensive, the men exhausted and troop numbers were dwindling rapidly due to enemy activity and the continuing epidemic of Spanish flu. Ludendorff issued orders for an attack to be made on 25 July by *First Army* against French positions west of Reims but on the same day as this took place with only limited success, there were further Allied attacks.

Withdrawal was now the only option and on 27 July troops started to move back to the Blücher Line. They initially stopped at the 'Big Bridgehead' line but this created too long a defensive line to hold and OHL ordered a full retirement to begin on the night of 1/2 August – the Blücher Movement. 'At 2pm on the 2nd August Soissons was evacuated, and at 2.30pm its bridges were blown up.' Fortunately there was little French interference and by 3 August all the troops were in place along the Blücher Line.

An analysis of recent events by OHL showed that there was a marked decline in troop morale due to too thin a defence line with insufficient depth, tiredness and shortage of food; as a result, where the French had successfully broken through, troops had surrendered en masse rather than continue to fight. On the other hand many units had fought well and in total the Allies had suffered considerably more casualties. As further proof of the general decline in morale, *Seventeenth Army* reported that new recruits were reluctant to fight. German troops, released from Russian POW camps, refused to fight on the Western Front and had to be organised into labour battalions to work at the front; many of them spread Bolshevik views about ending the Imperialist war. Allied intelligence reports showed a radical difference in the state of mind of the prisoners captured in March and July. 'The majority of those taken after 15 July retained only a much-shaken confidence' in the promises of success and of its being the last offensive.

Discipline was breaking down, with increasing numbers of attacks on superior officers, cases of insubordination, desertion and self-mutilation; crime was rampant; postal censors reported that many of the letters from front-line soldiers showed feelings of despondency about the war. There were also problems with the quality of the many new officers and NCOs, as well as a general shortage of men available for the army: for example, a quarter of the 1900 class who would be ready for the autumn campaigns were unfit for military service. On a personal level, despondency was increased by the chronically inadequate rations, shortage of beer, no leave, high civilian wages, the lack of medals for meritorious service and the poor army pay which was insufficient for the men who had to provide for families. Initially there was little problem with discipline in the front line; the everyday demands of life in the trenches made sure of this, but, by the time of the final offensives, there were signs that even there, discipline was being adversely affected.

Morale on the home front was also falling. Even though the press was strictly controlled, July 'newspapers contained such words as "the hour has come when the faith of the nation in the future and in victory requires to be sustained with a strong heart" and "it is the resistance of the nerves which will win the war".'

Despite declining morale, Ludendorff wanted Hagen to go ahead, 'whilst the defence is being organized, we must simultaneously prepare to attack.' With a withdrawal behind the River Vesle to regain operational freedom and OHL predictions that there would be no enemy attacks in the immediate future, the army needed to build divisions up to full strength and to rest the assault troops. Although Ludendorff told the Western Front Army commanders on 2 August that they were to go on the defensive (which the majority did not want to do) he still wanted a limited number of attacks to be made and, by 6 August, revised plans for Operations Elector and Hagen had been finalised. These limited attacks were to be surprise attacks in order to limit the number of casualties and to be defensive only.

During this period the Allies had been very quiet and on 5 August OHL received reports that *Second* and *Eighteenth Armies* were near to full strength and that morale was good. The next day *Second Army* launched an attack on British positions. While the gains were modest, one division (a *Würtemburger* division) successfully disrupted preparations for the forthcoming offensive, and, when they had dug in, severely hampered the ability of the British in that sector to keep up with other units in the 8 August attack.

The failure of the Reims offensive, according to Colonel Bauer, a close associate of Ludendorff, 'marked the tactical turning point in the war' and for Pétain the French successes, particularly on 18 July, 'had broken the spell'. The Allies now had the advantage and launched a major attack on 8 August that Ludendorff called a 'black day for the German Army'; after this there was no way to defeat the Entente powers – it was a matter of time and of what terms could be gained from a negotiated peace.

'On the Amiens front, German aircraft were forced back by 'a strong air barrage over and beyond our [the German] front line (that) prevented any observation into their [the British] rear areas.' The only sign of the impending attack that appears to have been noticed was that of the continuous movement of ammunition to the front areas in lorries. In some sectors the noise was interpreted as the movement of tanks, and concerns were raised about a tank attack on Villers-Bretonneux. By 6 August, reports about 100 tanks massing on the road from Ailly to Morisel caused anxiety in the front lines, but not among the staff. Captured British soldiers provided no information until some Royal Flying Corps 'officers stated on the 7th that a great attack was in preparation. Ludendorff was more concerned about the wave of defeatism that had come over the army. 'The troops 'were no longer *jauchzend* (shouting hurrah!), but had gone to the other extreme and were *zur Hölle betrübt* (depressed down to Hell).'

At 04.20 hrs on 8 August, Australian, British and Canadian troops, assisted by a devastating artillery bombardment, 800 aircraft and over 400 tanks, launched themselves at *Second Army*; by lunchtime 'the Allied success was virtually complete.' The speed and intensity of the fighting is described in the German *Official History*. 'Except for a local fight at Mezières the fate of the *225th Division* was settled about 10am...the *117th Division* suffered such heavy artillery fire that the Canadians were upon the front battalion, even into Marcelcave, before the troops could get out of their shelters...two of the three regimental staffs were captured...(the division) nearly quite shrunk to nothing, barely any infantry left. *41st*

Division attacked by 2nd Canadian and 2nd Australian Divisions suffered very heavily.' On the sector held by *13 Division*, about to be attacked by 3 Australian Division, 'the greater part of the defences shown on paper did not exist; it had only 27 out of its 36 field guns, 6 of which were early knocked out, and only 12 of its 36 heavy howitzers.' The division was shelled by artillery, attacked by infantry and attacked from the air, 'the situation was hopeless… the two battalions were broken and considerable parts surrounded, and had to lay down their arms.'

The official German account acknowledged that it was the greatest defeat since the start of the war with an estimated loss of up to 700 officers and 27,000 men, of whom about seventy percent were POWs. To paraphrase Churchill in the Second World War, it was the beginning of the end. It was not only under-strength and tired divisions that failed to hold the enemy advance: at Hangard Wood, a fresh full strength division collapsed when attacked by Canadian troops. After the war the Germans blamed the defeat on the unprepared defensive position which looked pretty on the map but in many cases merely amounted to a white tape on the ground to show where the line was supposed to be.

However, the British attacks next day were not as successful and many of the senior commanders did not accept Ludendorff's black day scenario; by the next day it was clear that the men were recovering from the initial shock of the attack and that resistance was stiffening, with the effect that the British advance was slowing down. Fortunately neither the British or the French were able to exploit their tactical success and the position stabilised for the German defenders. While casualties had been high, they were even higher for the attackers. The British *Official History* agreed with the senior German commanders and their appraisal of the first day of the offensive, 'on the face of it, the 8th August hardly seems to have deserved the fatal label of "the black day of the German Army".'

The question of morale was once again visited when casualty rates were analysed: sixty-nine percent of the casualties were missing, the majority assumed to have become POWs. Further evidence of failing morale was obvious when the *Alpen Korps,* having arrived in the battle area on 10 August, found, 'a chaos of scared men, loose horses and a confused block of vehicles' with troops both excited and fearful of renewed air attacks. It had become a case of every man for himself, with individuals and large parties 'wandering wildly about, but soon for the most part finding their way to the rear… the staff of the supply depots had fled, abandoning their stores… no one could give a clear idea of the actual position at the front… only here and there were a few isolated batteries in soldierly array, ready to support the reinforcing troops.' Within a week of the Allied attack, the number of unfit divisions had risen from 109 to 130.

At a meeting of the higher leaders at Avesnes, the HQ of both Hindenburg and Ludendorff, the latter declared, in the presence of the Kaiser, 'that a heavy defeat had been suffered, that the warlike spirit of some of the divisions left a good deal to be desired… troops falling back had shouted to one division as it came up the words "strike-breakers" and "War-mongers". The Kaiser then uttered the historic words: 'We have nearly reached the limit of our powers of resistance. The war must be ended.' During this period Crown Prince Rupprecht recorded in his memoirs that censored letters home revealed falling morale – 'It is time that our Government got peace, more and more Americans are coming out and we are having a foul time…too many hounds are the death of the hare. The war will end when the great capitalists have killed us all. You at home must strike, but make no mistake about it, and raise revolution, then peace will come. The air is literally poisoned by British airmen, so that we cannot understand where their newspapers get the stories of the heroic deeds of our aviators.'

The battle continued at a high cost to the German Army. Two weeks later a regiment of *107 Division* recorded that the fighting 'cost its old, good stock: all three battalion staffs, all company commanders, all medical officers and more than 600 men. Only two officers and 42 other ranks in addition to the regimental staff, escaped.' While the fighting was ferocious, the success of the enemy was not always due to fair tactics; *479 Regiment* accounted for its defeat – the British 'drove in front of them German prisoners who wore steel helmets, but who otherwise had taken off all their equipment.' To Ludendorff, 8 August was the black day for the German Army. To *234 Division,* it was 23 August when the British attackers 'broke in on both wings and killed or captured the greater part of the defenders: "the old *234th Division* was no more".

The history of *120 Württemburg Regiment* clearly illustrates that numerical superiority was now an overwhelming factor in the British advance. 'What took place on these days in the deep valley between the high ground at Bray, Suzanne and Maricourt could no longer be called a battle. The hostile brigades rolled forward behind a mighty curtain of fire and thoroughly smothered the very mixed-up German combatants, who had to defend themselves simultaneously against infantry, squadrons of tanks, cavalry, and aircraft. What did it matter if here and there our guns blew up a tank, if our machine guns shot an attacking cavalry detachment to pieces, if our fighter aeroplanes shot down several hostile machines? The enemy filled the gaps in the twinkling of an eye, but the brave body of Württemburgers and their helpers got weaker hour by hour… . When on the 25 August the regimental commander, on orders from division, assembled the regiment near Curlu he saw before him just one company not quite at war establishment strength, that is to say two hundred and fifty souls [instead of 3,000] amongst whom were only a few officers.'

There were also significant losses in materiel. *116 Regiment* suffered heavily during the British attack up 'Happy Valley' and reported that 'almost everything was lost'. Any withdrawal would exacerbate the loss of materiel because there was insufficient time to remove it to any reserve positions. In an attempt to address some of the advantages the Entente had in men and materiel, it was decided that all railway lines must be destroyed, to slow down their advance and to provide time for a withdrawal. On 26 August, orders were given for the retirement of *Second* and *Eighteenth* Armies 'to a shorter line from Noyon along the east bank of the canal to Nesle, and thence along the Somme to the north-west of Péronne' on the night of 27-28 August.

The position the German Army found itself in was summed up by General Schwarte: 'During the four days 30th August – 2nd September the Allied Powers attacked unceasingly on a front of approximately ninety miles from Arras to Soissons. They were in a position to keep on throwing fresh and well-rested divisions into the battle. The development of air fighting was great, and low-flying aeroplanes in large numbers took part in the attacks'. Many blamed the failure of the defence on the low effectiveness of many of the units involved – units that were not only under-strength but also exhausted. Positions were weakened when their troops made off before the relief troops arrived.

Further withdrawals were planned to shorten the line. On the Home Front the situation was also deteriorating. 'Crown Prince Rupprecht, who was returning to the front from sick leave, recorded in his diary: 'In Nürnberg the inscription on a troop train read "Slaughter cattle for Wilhelm & Sons"'.

A month after the start of the Amiens battle, three Entente Army groups were ready to strike: the Americans in the south, the British in the north, and the French in the centre. However, it would not be a rout, even though there was a shortage of equipment, horses and men. The Americans found this out when they tried to take the St. Mihiel salient, where both the topography and the defensive layout favoured the defenders. Even though the German defenders were outnumbered, it took the attacking American and French troops a month to break through the Meuse-Argonne defences and in achieving this victory the American forces incurred nearly forty percent of their total casualties for the war – 117,000 against German losses of about 80,000.

'As the allied attacks gathered momentum on several sectors throughout August and September, the army began to dissolve' – and Crown Prince Rupprecht noted in his diary at the end of September that it was unlikely that *Fourth Army* would stand up to a serious attack. To further emphasise the severity of the situation, at a meeting on 29 September at Spa, having given an account of the military situation, Ludendorff stated, according to Admiral Hintze, the Foreign Minister, that 'the situation of the Army demands an immediate armistice in order to save a catastrophe'. When the Chancellor arrived at the meeting, he was deeply perturbed by the request for an armistice. He tendered his resignation; it was accepted. On 1 October, Ludendorff asked Prince Max of Baden to form a government otherwise Ludendorff himself would ask for an armistice. The next day Major von der Bussche, Ludendorff's liaison

The elite of the army – Stormtroopers with their distinctive shoulder bags for carrying extra grenades.

Two soldiers paying their respects to a fallen comrade in a captured French cemetery with 1917 burials.

The debris of war – a destroyed British truck with half buried occupant.

A destroyed British field gun near Rumilly.

officer with the Reichstag, summarised the military situation to the party leaders, and told them that the war was lost, that every twenty-four hours would only worsen the situation.

With the continued Allied attacks it was considered prudent to retire to supposedly prepared positions. Boehn's group of Armies, based north and south of St. Quentin, was particularly vulnerable. 'Owing to lack of reserves, it was considered that the only possible course was to yield ground bit by bit and defend every yard, in the expectation that the enemy's losses and the German political proposals would gradually cause the hostile attacks to weaken.' There could be no grand retirement as the Hermann positions were not complete; the problem was further compounded by troop exhaustion, the enormous loss of army stores and irreplaceable local supplies.

At the front, as morale dropped, desertions increased, and troops became ever less reliable, putting their ability to sustain the defensive in doubt. However, there remained some reliable troops who provided resistance until the very end of the war. During this period the wholesale surrender of units indicated a lack of will to continue the fight. Hundreds of thousands of men escaped further combat by disappearing rearwards or feigning light injury or sickness in what has been called a 'covert military strike'. The story was basically the same along the whole of the Western Front. By early October, the Hindenburg line had been breached and the German Army had pulled back over fifty miles; the outcome was no longer in doubt. By 8 October the battalions were reporting that their numbers were down to an average of 150 men of all ranks – and that these survivors were completely burned out.

The gravity of the position became clear to the troops at the front when they received the Order of the Day to the German Army and Navy, on 5 October, from the Kaiser. After describing their struggle against superior numbers and the collapse of the Macedonian Front it ended thus: 'Your front is unbroken and will remain so. In agreement with my Allies I have decided to offer peace once more to our enemies; but we will only stretch out our hands for an honourable peace.' On the same day the new Chancellor 'announced that a step had been made towards peace'. On the Home Front 'the Chancellor's armistice approach sent a wave of relief and hope through Germany'.

But the war continued with systematic deportation and destruction as the troops retreated, and, when a U-boat sank two British passenger ships with the loss of over eight hundred lives, President Wilson rejected the proposals. The Minister of War pointed out that what was being offered amounted to an unconditional surrender. Once again civilians returned to what had become the norm: depression and gloom. Rumours circulated in an atmosphere of alarm and uncertainty. Each day brought further signs of demoralisation and the threat of disorder. In order to reinforce the front, the Minister of War advised Ludendorff that, by calling up the 1900 class and combing out industry, he could provide a further 600,000 men; this offer was refused at first but, two days later, he was told to get them ready as soon as possible.

On 15 October, President Wilson demanded preliminary conditions that were impossible for OHL to fulfil, even if it had wanted to. The war would continue while the diplomatic discussions continued; the reality was that the army had to continue to hold as much enemy territory as possible to use as a lever in any future discussions. When President Wilson demanded the end of U-boat warfare as a precursor to an armistice, Ludendorff alone would not concur. Eventually, under the pretext that OHL had no political responsibility, he washed his hands of the matter. The conditions were then agreed on.

Crown Prince Rupprecht, on the same day, described the military situation as he saw it in a letter to Prince Max: 'Our troops are exhausted and their numbers have dwindled terribly. The number of infantry in an Active division is seldom as much as 3,000 – in certain cases is only equivalent to two or three companies. Quantities of machine guns have been lost and there is a lack of trained machine-gun teams. The artillery has also lost a great number of guns and suffers from a lack of trained gun-layers. In certain Armies fifty per cent of the guns are without horses. There is also a lack of ammunition… the morale of the troops has suffered seriously and their power of resistance diminishes daily. They surrender in hordes, whenever the enemy attacks, and thousands of plunderers infest the districts around the bases.' It was not just a shortage of men, guns and ammunition. He continued: 'We have no more prepared lines, and no more can be dug. There is a shortage of fuel for the lorries, and when the Austrians desert us, and we get no more petrol from Rumania, two months will put a stop to our aviation.' There were insufficient reserves to hold a full attack and, even if the army retreated behind the Meuse, it would only be a temporary hold on the retreat, especially as the retreating army was leaving behind equipment that could not be replaced. While the German Army was running out of men, the Americans were arriving in ever-increasing numbers. He finished his letter with three simple statements: 'I do not believe there is any possibility of holding out over December', that the 'situation is already exceedingly dangerous, and that under certain circumstances a catastrophe can occur overnight' so 'we must obtain peace before the enemy breaks through into Germany'. He was also concerned about Ludendorff as the commander in chief, because he felt that he 'does not realize the whole seriousness of the situation'. On 23 October, during a debate in the Reichstag, 'it was held that Ludendorff's suggestions were unsatisfactory' and that he should offer his resignation. In reply, on 25 October, Ludendorff issued an Order of the Day to the press but not to the government: 'Wilson's answer means military capitulation. It is therefore unacceptable to us soldiers. When the enemy realises that German front is not broken through… he will be ready for a peace which ensures Germany's future.' The press regarded this as a stab in the back, an idea to be used later for different means.

Ludendorff then decided to go to Berlin, report to the Kaiser and demand that President Wilson's terms be rejected. 'The Chancellor now made up his mind that Ludendorff must be dismissed'. After a discussion with the Kaiser about the military and political situation Ludendorff offered his resignation, which was accepted, although Hindenburg's resignation was not accepted. That evening Austria-Hungary asked Italy for an armistice. On 31 October, Turkey bowed out of the war.

Towards the end of October, evidence of the state of feeling in the Army, the Navy and the Homeland had become too obvious to ignore or conceal. On 30 October, *18 Landwehr Division* had refused to go into the trenches in Lorraine, and there were signs of disaffection in other divisions; on 2 November, the reinforcements from the Russian Front for the *Seventeenth Army* mutinied and had to be disarmed by a Storm battalion, and its Chief of Staff stated that it would not stand another attack. In the back areas wandered thousands of deserters and marauders.

While the army retreated, mutiny broke out among the sailors at Kiel in response to orders to put to sea. The revolt spread quickly to Bremen, Cuxhaven, Hamburg and Lübeck, followed by riots in Coblenz, Cologne, Düsseldorf and Mainz; large numbers of army deserters arriving from the front helped fuel the flames of discontent. There were mass marches and processions in Berlin and everywhere the cry was 'The Kaiser must go'. When the Chancellor announced the Kaiser's abdication, there was wild rejoicing in Berlin. Red flags replaced the traditional Hohenzollern flag.

The cost of defeat was high. In the last nine months of the war, over one million men had been lost and of these nearly 400,000 had been taken prisoner since 18 July. On 11 November the war came to end with an armistice, and the Germans left the occupied territories, followed closely by their enemy. Although the German Army left the Western Front there were many men who stayed behind. These would be there for some considerable time as POWs, and some of them would return in just over twenty years' time – this time as the victors.

British POWs being escorted to the rear while German reinforcements make their way to the front.

A mobile British machine gun post after being hit by a shell.

A visit by The Kaiser to the Western Front.

German defensive fortications overlooking french postions in the Champagne.

A British casualty of the offensive – a corporal in a trench mortar section (note the trench mortar ammunition in the top left). This soldier has a wound stripe on his left forearm.

Hindenburg handing out medals during the offensive.

The remains of a British artillery column after being shelled.

Second wave troops wait to advance.

A British heavy artillery piece caught in the open – note that both corpses have been searched and their boots taken.

A captured British rifle being set to fire on its original owners using a lever.

A heavy British artillery piece captured by the fast-moving storm troops. This gun is named 'Persuader'.

French POWs being escorted by cavalry – note the pre-war headgear worn by the mounted troops (behind the lines such headgear, along with picklehaubes continued to be worn until the end of the war).

Both sides used balloons to help with reconnaissance and artillery spotting. This German observation balloon has a single observer. Balloons were easy targets for passing fighter aircraft and observers were given parachutes.

13389

Moving field guns forward to keep in touch with the advance was not always an easy job.

A field conference just before the attack.

British officers arriving at a Pow camp in Germany after their capture in the March offensive.

egsbilder aus Frankreich. 9

Der Veterinär bei der Arbeit.

Phot. A. Menzen Berlin.

Horse drawn transport was essential for re-supply of the advancing troops but there were never enough horses and as the war continued their physical condition declined.

Soldiers at rest awaiting their turn to be called to the front.

Troops advancing through an artillery barrage.

The propaganda view of the man at the front.

The loss of von Richoften (seated) was great blow to morale.

Horse transport of 6 *Garde Regiment*.

Light artillery such as this field piece was camouflaged to hide it from the air. There was no time to dig the guns in as the advance was often very rapid.

A restful occupation when not in the front line – painting steel helmets.

The OHL had little faith in tanks and did not order their mass production, probably because the German A7V was markedly inferior to the British tank. Here Adalbert is being transported to the front.

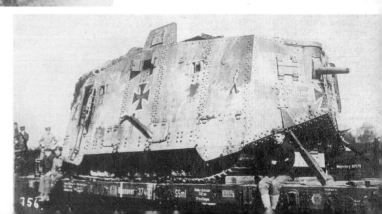

A knocked-out British tank.

A British lorry destroyed by shell fire during the early stages of the Operation Michael.

A youthful stormtrooper complete with grenade bag, automatic pistol, binoculars and flare pistol.

British artillery captured during the advance.

Heavy French artillery – a response to the German Big Bertha guns.

Youthful recruits of *Landwehr Regiment 606* from Army district 7, in training.

A modified field gun in use as an anti-aircraft weapon.

A communications wagon for field telephones.

The Kaiser was so pleased with the progress of the war that he gave medals to both Hindenburg and Ludendorff – many senior officers felt he was being presumptuous and that he should have waited to reward them when the war was over.

A German Unteroffizier behind the lines opposite French troops.

British POWs and German troops in a hospital at Heilbronn.

A unit marches to the front – some of the troops are wearing the Model 1918 cut out helmet favoured by cavalry and specialised infantry units.

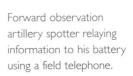

Forward observation artillery spotter relaying information to his battery using a field telephone.

A well dug-in heavy trench mortar.

British field artillery captured during the offensive.

First aid in a quiet area of the front carried out by medics at the aid post.

This photo clearly shows the problems of transport in wet weather away from main roads.

Troops undergoing training in a rear area while enjoying a period of rest.

Whether the soldier survived is not indicated on the this photo — eight metres from the enemy. French sap post in the wood near Apremont.

The army was suffering from shortages of lots of basic materials, one of which was rubber. This shows some of the arrangements made to replace the rubber on truck tyres.

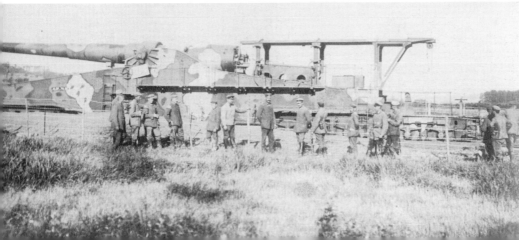

French railway gun captured near Vailly.

A heavy artillery piece manufactured by Krupps being transported for finishing off.

Life on the Home Front - a wooden statue of Hindenburg which became the Iron Man when people hammered nails into it after a charitable donation.

The war on the Eastern Front was over but it was to have a lasting effect on many of the troops that served there. Here Russians and Germans fraternise during the winter of 1917. Many of the troops selected for service on the Western Front brought communist ideas and ideals with them.

Heavy fighting resulted in heavy casualties – a German mortuary on the Western Front.

The Schneider CA.1 was the first French tank, and possibly the worst AFV of the whole war. It was painfully slow, badly ventilated, cramped and noisy and its armour was thin - but the same can be said of almost all tanks of the Great War. In addition to these problems, it used a standard Holt Tractor track system, which was far too short for this kind of vehicle, making trench-crossing and parapet-climbing very difficult.

Armament was another problem; its main gun was located in a small embrasure on the right hand side, with a very narrow field of fire as a result - the two MGs were also mounted in an awkward way that limited their usefulness.

However, the tank's largest drawback were the two petrol tanks placed high up like the British Mk 1. The engine had no fuel pump and depended on gravity feed. The side armour was often penetrated - which happened easily: it was so thin that shell splinters could puncture the fuel tanks, spraying the crew with petrol. As a result, a simple, misplaced bullet could set the whole tank on fire – and so it was nicknamed "The Mobile Crematorium".

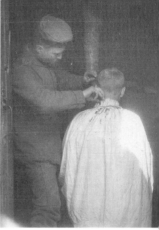

Even with a war going on men needed haircuts.

Landwehr infantry marching to the front accompanied by their band.

A German dummy gun in the field to attract enemy fire.

A trench in the woods somewhere on the Western Front.

A destroyed British tank from 2 Battalion Tank Corps.

A Bavarian theatrical troop in uniform and above in stage clothes.

An off-duty moment at the Kantine when there were stocks to be had.

There might have been a war on, but there were still civilians around.

Troops massing before moving to the front. In the foreground is a light machine gun.

The late 1918 fighting man.

A well dug-in heavy trench mortar.

A German ammunition dump at Vigneulles after a direct hit from French artillery.

Trench style humour – I didn't want the war; I'm not aware of being guilty; nor me; Wilson sent me; stupid me; and me too.

Joseph Keilhofer, a Bavarian soldier killed in action on 15 July 1918.

Reaping the benefits of someone else's work.

Flamethrower troops move forward.

Flamethrowers in action.

Two brothers, August (KIA on 22 May 1918) and Joseph Stürmlinger (KIA on 8 August 1918).

Even with a war on, there was woodcutting to be done in the rear areas.

A lorry-mounted anti-aircraft gun that could also be used against tanks.

Enemy aircraft alert – soldiers leaving their supply column in a practice.

June 1918 – a busy railhead. Judging by the number of parcels the troops have, it is probable that they are returning to the front after leave.

A dead artillery man after a British barrage.

French POWs taken in April 1918 – note the unusual gun held by the guard at the right of the picture.

A dead soldier after a British barrage.

A British trench after a successful German attack.

As most bridges had been blown up by the retreating soldiers, it was necessary to construct pontoon bridges to allow troop movement.

American troops enjoying a meal at a French restaurant before moving to the front.

Soldiers called up in April/May 1918 gather for a group photo before shipping out to the front.

An artillery dump near Péronne during 1918.

Heavily camouflaged field artillery somewhere on a French plain.

August 1918 Tug-of-war competition for *249 Infantry Regiment* while out on rest.

Ceremonial march past to help keep morale up.

Life continued in the villages behind the lines for both soldier and civilian alike.

Conventional railways could not get material close to the front line, so hundreds of miles of narrow gauge track were laid to move stores quickly and easily and often without the need for a locomotive.

Although they were far too small or too big for infantry service in the trenches, both men were members of *31 Infantry Regiment*.

Members of a machine gun unit (note the badge on the arm) having fun.

Winning hearts and minds – a
regimental band playing for
the civilian population.

The Geneva
convention forbids the
carrying of weapons
by medics – here each
soldier is carrying an
automatic pistol.

A suitable soldier's comment on the situation.

Some of the many German soldiers who stayed behind on the Western Front as POWs in France.

Chronology of the Western Front
1917-1918

1917

1 January. Successful raid captures Hope Post from British. A further 50 infantry gun batteries formed for anti-tank use.

2 January. General Mudra takes over command of Army Detachment A in Lorraine.

5 January. Two posts captured near Beaumont Hamel by the British.

9 January. Trenches east of Beaumont Hamel lost to British.

16 January. British daylight trench raid west of Lens.

17 January. Daylight raid by the British on trenches west of Lens. Four counterattack fail to eject the British troops who had captured 600 yards of trench north of Beaumont-sur-Ancre.

21 January. Attacks north of Bois de Caurières near Verdun repulsed by the French.

25 January. Success at Hill 304; mile long stretch of French trenches stormed but mostly lost to counterattack.

27 January. 350 strong garrison lost to British attack near Le Transloy.

28 January. Crown Prince Rupprecht demands a voluntary retirement to the Siegfried Stellung as a result of the British pressure on the Ancre. Retirement vetoed by German OHL.

30 January. French trench raid south of Leintrey in Lorraine reaches 2nd line and takes POWs.

31 January. counterattack on British positions on the Ancre repulsed. BEF claims over 1200 POWs taken during January.

1 February. Fifteen battalions and two companies of Stosstruppen (shock troops) serving on the Western Front. Each Infantry Company is to be provided with three light machine guns (Bergmann LMG) as soon as possible. British positions near Wytschaete (Wijtschate) and Grandcourt unsuccessfully raided. British trench raid near Gueudcourt takes 56 POWs. Senior commanders and staffs attend Solesmes tactical school to learn new defence methods.

3 February. British advance 500 yards east of Beaucourt taking over 100 prisoners.

4 February. Operation Alberich authorised by the Kaiser: retirement to Siegfried Stellung; 65 miles long with average depth of 19 miles; whole area given the scorched earth treatment. Objective: release thirteen divisions and shorten front by twenty-five miles.

6 February. Grandcourt evacuated after British occupy 1000 yards of trenches.

8 February. Hill 153 (Sailly-Saillsel ridge) lost to British troops along with 78 POWs.

9 February. Attacks on the Meuse repulsed by French. Operation Alberich commences: demolitions and programmed removal of material and civilian population.

10 February. Counterattack fails to regain 1250-yard trench system south of Serre Hill from the British; 215 POWs lost during initial attack.

11 February. 600 yards of trenches near Beaucourt-Puisieux road lost to British.

12 February. Successful British trench raid south of Souchez.

13 February. Forty POWs lost to British trench raiders northeast of Arras.

14 February. North-west of Compiègne French troops make a trench raid.

15 February. Raid on British trenches near Loos, west of Messines and northeast of Ypres. Attack on French salient west of Maisons de Champagne gains trenches and takes 858 POWs.

17 February. French raid on salient northeast of Altkirch causes heavy loss. British attacks at Miraumont result in 773 POWs and up to 1000 yards' loss of front during the two attacks.

Franz Marchl - killed in action on
15 January 1917.

A British trench after the attack
had moved on.

Naval garrison
troops of
Batterie Tirpitz
at Westende on
the Belgian
coast.

18 February. Attacks on British positions above Baillescourt Farm repulsed.

19 February. 114 POWs lost during British raid east of Ypres. South of Le Transloy, attacks with flamethrowers captures British post and 30 POWs.

22 February. Retirement to Siegfried Stellung accelerated due to British pressure, with a preliminary withdrawal of three miles on a fifteen-mile frontage.

25 February. General Sixt von Arnim takes over *Fourth Army* from Duke Albrecht of Württemburg who is given command of Flanders Army Group. British and Australian attacks on Les Thilloys (south-west of Bapaume) until 2 March.

27 February. Villages of Ligny and Le Barque on the Somme lost to British attacks; successful British trench raid east of Armentières.

28 February. Over the month British attacks resulted in the loss of eleven villages and 2133 POWs.

1 March. Reorganisation: Arnim's *Fourth Army* on the Belgian coast becomes part of Rupprecht's Army Group. Army detachments on left flank of Rupprecht's troops previously formed into new Army Group under Albrecht. Seventh Army transferred from Rupprecht's group to Crown Prince William's Army Group. Battalion strength reduced to 750 from around 1080 but now 1422 battalions – 1289 during September 1916.

2 March. counterattack near Bapaume fail to hold Les Thilloys; further territory lost north-west of Puisieux and north of Warlencourt.

3 March. *51 (Reserve) Division* raid south of Ripont on French lines captures memo on future general Allied offensive but loses territory east of Gommecourt.

4 March. Bouchavesnes lost to British 8 Division with 217 POWs; six counterattack fail to regain village. 28 Division penetrates Caurières Wood on the Verdun Front.

5 March. Attack launched west of Pont-à-Mousson in Lorraine.

8 March. French attack on Butte de Mesnils – Maisons de Champagne regains most of the salient lost on 15 February. Five raids made on British trenches around Messines.

10 March. Irles and Grévillers Trench lost along with 292 POWs.

11 March. General Fuchs replaces General Boehn as commander of Army Detachment C, Boehn takes command of *Seventh Army*.

12 March. Small rearguard parties protect evacuating troops around Péronne. On the Aisne Front, artillery shells Soissons with incendiaries. Rettemoy Graben (trench) attacked by British 46 Division.

13 March. Attack on Hill 185 repulsed by French troops. Further territory lost to British east and north-east of Gommecourt.

14 March. Main retreat to the Siegfried Stellung begins with British following cautiously.

15 March. British advance between St. Pierre Vaast Wood and Sallisel on a 1½ mile front and further south French troops begin their advance.

16 March. Synchronised retreat to Siegfried Stellung begun by thirty-five divisions; St. Pierre Vaast wood occupied by British troops.

17 March. Bapaume occupied by 2 Australian Division; BEF occupies a total of thirteen villages and French occupy Roye.

18 March. French repulse attacks at Avocourt-Mort Homme on Verdun sector. Allies enter Nesle together while French enter Noyon and the BEF enters Chaulnes and Péronne.

19 March. Retreat completed by twenty-nine divisions.

20 March In order to stop its use as an observation post, medieval castle of Couchy-le-Château is demolished. British begin preparatory barrage for April offensive at Arras.

21 March French overcome resistance on Crozat Canal and take Tergnier.

23 March. Oise valley deliberately flooded.

24 March. Roisel, east of Péronne, occupied by British troops.

25 March. Reims shelled.

26 March. Lagnicourt lost to Australian attack along with about fifty POWs. French pressure pushes troops back to the Barisis-Servais line with the loss of Coucy-le-Château.

27 March. French forces reach Aisne-Oise canal near Soissons.

28 March. Hill 304 at Verdun lost to French attack.

30 March. In Cambrai area, British occupy a further eight villages.

1 April. City of Reims shelled by a barrage of 25,000 rounds. Troops pushed back to Vauxaillon by French attack. Savy and Savy Wood lost to British attacks.

2 April. Air attacks and weather hamper French range-finding and counter-battery work. Further British pressure between Arras and St. Quentin results in the loss of nine villages, 700 killed and 240 POWs to the attacking troops.

3 April. French occupy seven villages near St. Quentin in the Somme region.

4 April. British 2000-gun artillery barrage along twelve-mile front at Arras. Raiding party at Mount Sapigneul captures divisional orders giving movements of 3 Corps on right of French Fifth Army.

5 April. Allied movements impeded by rearguard actions, booby traps, demolitions and the weather but majority of troops now in the Siegfried Stellung.

8 April. City of Reims shelled.

9 April. At 0530 in bitter cold and sleet the British attack on a twelve-mile front at Arras, breaching the third line defences, capturing 5600 POWs and thirty-six guns in an advance varying from 2000 to 6000 yards. After an attack by the Canadian Corps, only the north end of Vimy ridge is held; five villages lost along with 4000 POWs and fifty-four guns.

10 April. Hill 145 on Vimy Ridge lost to Canadian attack but reserves seal gap in Arras front. French shell positions on Moronvillers massif near Reims.

11 April. Monchy-le-Preux and Wancourt lost to tank and infantry attack but Allied infantry and tanks repulsed at Bullecourt taking 1170 Allied POWs and capturing two tanks.

12 April. Pimple Hill stormed by Canadian infantry.

13 April. Villages of Vimy and Petit Vimy lost to Canadian attack. Heavy fighting at Wancourt Ridge but line held until 15 April. Further south French Army held and attack called off.

14 April. Ten British soldiers hold Monchy-le-Preux against attacks from *3 Bavarian Division* for five hours.

15 April Four-division attack on a seven-mile front at Lagnicourt repulsed by the Anzac Corps and British 62 Division.

16 April. Twenty-division French attack on the Aisne Front contained with heavy casualties by fifteen divisions. Thirty-two tanks knocked out and French advance about 600 yards.

17 April. Moronvillers attacked by French troops. Four villages evacuated and burned south of Chemin des Dames.

18 April. Villers Guislain and Gonnelieu to British attacks. Counterattack near Juvincourt repulsed by the French even though many French units in a state of unrest.

19 April. Fort Condé on the Aisne Front lost to French attack and road on Chemin des Dames secured by French. In the Champagne region, Aubérive lost to determined attack by the French Foreign Legion.

20 April. French Aisne offensive ceases but over 16,000 POWs lost during the attacks.

21 April. Further French attacks on the Aisne between Hurtebise and Berry-au-Bac. Limited territorial losses on the Somme due to 40th British Division attack.

22 April. General Falkenhausen replaced as commander of Sixth Army by General Below.

23 April. Troops pushed back after a British nine division assault on a nine-mile front across the River Scarpe. Guémappe lost, five counterattack fail to take Gavrelle and 2500 POWs lost to the defenders. Heavy casualties inflicted on the attacking British troops.

28 April. Village of Arleux taken by Canadian attack along with 450 POWs but, further south, at Oppy, three British divisions held, inflicting heavy casualties including 475 British POWs.

29 April. Some trenches lost between Oppy and Gavrelle.

1 May. counterattack and raids on French positions south of Moronvillers repulsed. Infantry companies receive two Bergmann LMGs. Losses fighting the British at Arras since 9 April include over 18,000 POWs, over 450 guns and mortars, 470 machine guns and a territorial loss on a twenty-mile front of between two and five miles in depth, against British losses of just under 84,000 casualties.

A close-up of the basket for an observer under an observation balloon.

3 May. Fourteen British divisions attack east of Arras for little gain although Fresnoy captured by the Canadians. Further south Australian and British forces break through the Siegfried Stellung at Quéant.

4 May. Craonne and trenches on a three-mile front northwest of Reims lost to French assault.

5 May. Craonne Ridge, including Chemin des Dames and Laffaux Mill, as well as 6000 POWs, lost to French assault using 48 tanks. All counterattacks repulsed.

6 May. Counterattack near River Souchez repulsed by British.

7 May. Troops move back between Bullecourt and Quéant as a result of Australian attack.

8 May. On the second attack 5 Bavarian Division recaptures Fresnoy near Arras. On the Aisne front, despite counterattacks, the French take the trenches near Chevreux.

9 May. Counterattacks fail to take Chemin des Dames, Craonne and Corbény.

10 May. Troops fall back on south bank of the Scarpe after British attack.

11 May. Despite repeated counterattacks by *80 (Reserve) Division*, Canadian troops hold 300 yards of trenches west of Avion. Cavalry Farm, Chemical Works and Roeux captured by the British.

12 May. Most of Bullecourt falls to British.

13 May. Counterattacks against French positions north of Reims and in Maison de Champagne fail. British push forward on Greenland Hill.

14 May. Trench raids against French positions on the Aisne and in Champagne. North of Gavrelle troops pushed back by British attack.

15 May. Heavy fighting against the British around Bullecourt and against the French on Chemin des Dames. The French raid trenches in the Woëvre and Lorraine.

An infantry section pose for the camera in January 1917.

A wooded rest area behind the lines.

Malerische Unterstände

16 May. Counterattacks against the British at Gavrelle fail. The Battle of Arras results in the loss of sixty-one square miles of territory, nearly 21,000 POWs and over 250 guns.

18 May. Attacks on Chemin des Dames repulsed by French but troops retake 200 yards of California Plateau.

20 May. First line of the Siegfried Stellung north of Bullecourt lost to British 33 Division, and 500 POWs taken by the French during attacks in the Moronvillers sector.

21 May. Troops pull back against British attacks at Fontaine-les-Croisilles.

22 May. French successfully raid trenches on the Aisne Front.

23 May. Dawn raid against French positions on Vauclère Plateau unsuccessful, but some slight gains made round Craonne and Mount Cornillet near Moronvillers.

25 May. Attack against French positions near Braye on Chemin des Dames successful.

26 May. Counterattacks against the French in the Champagne region fail.

27 May. Small scale fighting on the Alsace, Champagne and Verdun fronts.

28 May. Attempt to regain territory around Hubertise, lost to the French on 20 April, fails.

29 May. Skirmishing with British troops near St. Quentin and patrol activity in the Champagne region.

30 May. French repel heavy attacks on Moronvillers Massif.

31 May. Artillery duels with British around Ypres for a week.

1 June. Ten divisions transferred from the Lens-Lille sector to Flanders. French positions on the Aisne Front raided at dawn.

3 June. After a 600-projector gas barrage, Canadian troops assault but cannot hold La Coulette; 100 POWs lost to attacking forces. French successfully repel five attacks against Chemin des Dames and one near Hubertise. As a result of feint, British artillery barrage guns drawn into counter-battery retaliation shelling.

5 June. Some positions lost on Greenland Hill due to British attack.

7 June. Messines-Wytschaete Ridge lost as a result of British attack on a nine-mile wide front that was preceded by the detonation of nineteen mines simultaneously (the largest non-nuclear explosion recorded); panic in Lille fifteen miles from the explosion. Gruppe Wytschaete Commander Laffert dismissed from post and 6400 POWs lost.

8 June. Counterattacks against British positions east of Messines Ridge repulsed. As British troops continue to advance, troops withdrawn to a new defensive line running through Warneton. A very strong raid by Canadian troops, west of Avion, takes more than 150 POWs and inflicts over 830 casualties.

13 June. General Pershing arrives at Boulogne.

14 June. Positions on Infantry Hill successfully attacked by 3 Australian Infantry Division.

15 June. Counterattack southeast of Ypres repulsed by British. Troops fail to hold British near Bullecourt.

17 June. Portuguese Expeditionary Corps in action in Flanders. French repulse attack on Mount Le Téton and advance between Mounts Cornillet and Blond.

18 June. Counterattack dislodges Australian troops at Infantry Hill.

20 June. Australians regain Infantry Hill and repulse attacks on the River Souchez after initial gains, while attacks against the French near Vauxaillon and Filain take and hold ground.

21 June. Gains made at Vauxaillon on 20 June mostly lost to French counterattack. British begin operations on the Flanders coast.

22 June. Some of the gains made at Filain lost to the French.

24 June. British night attack results in retreat from River Souchez positions. French attack at Filain restores positions to those held on 19 June.

25 June. Dragon's Cave, near Hubertise on Chemin des Dames, taken by French troops.

26 June. Advance troops of US 1 Infantry Division land at St. Nazaire. British occupy La Coulotte and Canadian Corps begins capture of Avion.

27 June. Long Max (15 inch gun) fires fifty-five shells at Dunkirk, twenty-four miles from its position at Luegenboom.

28 June. During fierce fighting west of Hill 304 and Mort Homme, in the Verdun region, some trenches captured from the French. Heavy fighting the Artois region results in the loss of Hill 65, a two mile stretch south of the River Souchez, most of Avion and an edge of Oppy Wood. 14,000 US regulars and marines land at St. Nazaire.

29 June. Attacks against French positions around Cerny on Chemin des Dames.

30 June. High Command learns of French mutinies.

1 July In Artois the British attack Liévin and the French counterattack northwest of Mort Homme near Verdun.

3 July. Large-scale attack on an eleven-mile front north of the Aisne against the French.

5 July. Slight advance made south of Ypres by British troops.

6 July. 300,000 high explosive and gas shells fired against new British positions at the Yser bridgeheads.

7 July. Minor French gains on the Aisne and at Verdun.

8 July. Counterattacks on the Aisne repulsed by the French.

9 July. Counterattacks on the Aisne against French positions repulsed while French counterattack at Bray-en-Launnois. In the Flanders sector British advance slightly near Messines.

10 July. Dawn attack by fifteen battalions against Nieuport defences. Marines advance near Lombaertzyde on a 1400-yard front east of the mouth of the River Yser, surrounding two British platoons that fight to the last man. Other attacks in the sector held or repulsed.

12 July. 50,000 rounds of Mustard gas fired at British positions around Ypres.

14 July. In the Champagne region, French attacks on the Moronvillers Massif capture trenches that are held against all counterattacks. On the Aisne Front small gains are made against the French at Cerny and on Chemin des Dames.

17 July. British begin bombardment prior to offensive at Ypres. French regain positions north-west of Mort Homme lost to German action over the previous eighteen days. Trench raids made against French positions northwest of Verdun all unsuccessful.

18 July. Trench raids southwest of St. Quentin repulsed by British.

19 July. Further attacks in Nieuport, north Aisne and St. Quentin sectors.

22 July. French retake ground lost during heavy fighting in the north Aisne sector. Trench raids against French positions near Verdun unsuccessful.

23 July *36 (Reserve) Division* loses 53 POWs during Canadian trench raid.

24 July French repulse attacks north of the River Aisne and at Mount Haut in Champagne region.

27 July. Counterattack to reclaim 3000 yards of evacuated trenches beaten off by British Guards Division.

31 July. At 03.50 hrs British and French attack on a fifteen-mile front from the River Yser to the River Lys. counterattack successfully restrict the Allied advance but over 5000 men lost as POWs. Small losses to the French troops, west of Chevregny on the Aisne Front. Two battalions attack French positions on the Cerney Plateau after five-minute bombardment.

1 August. St. Julien recaptured from British with further gains made near the Ypres-Roulers rail line, but French make gains on west bank of the Yser Canal.

2 August. Gains on the Ypres-Roulers rail line lost to British attack. Waterlogged shell holes
start to appear on the Ypres Front. Battle line on Pilckem Ridge now up to 3000 yards back from the start of the attack, but nearly 32,000 British casualties inflicted. Some British trenches stormed and held on Infantry Hill near Monchy-le-Preux.

3 August. Severe casualties inflicted upon attacking British troops and the defenders but St. Julien lost as well as any gains on Infantry Hill from 2 August. Allied attacks on the Scarpe successfully held.

5 August. After initial success against positions near Hollebeke, troops pushed back.

8 August. Ground lost to a French attack northwest of Bixschoote.

10 August. Westhoek and Glencorse Wood lost to British attack on a two-mile front east of Ypres. Inverness Copse lost, but troops hold onto some positions on the Gheluvelt Plateau. Further ground lost to French attacks east and north of Bixschoote.

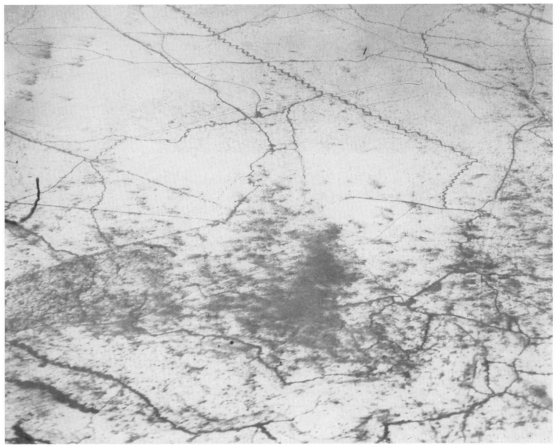

An aerial view of the snow covered trenches near Chaulnes on 8 February 1917. (note the dark patches caused by the heavy bombardment throwing up earth).

German POWs in French hands – note PG on the tunic standing for Prisonnier de Guerre.

11 August. Successful counterattack east of Ypres recaptures part of Glencorse wood.

13 August. Heavy French bombardment on positions along a 12½ mile front at Verdun. In reply one million Mustard gas shells fired on French positions over the next ten days.

15 August. Hill 70 north of Lens and five nearby villages lost to Canadian attack with heavy casualties on both sides; over 1100 POWs taken by attackers.

16 August. British attack on a nine-mile front north of the Ypres-Menin road results in the loss of Langemarck and troops pulling back across the River Steenbeck. Counterattacks regain some of the ground but push two British divisions back to their start line. Drie Grachten bridgehead on the Yser Canal lost to a French Marine battalion. Further south, on the Aisne, some territory lost to the French attack on the Craonne Plateau. Some French trenches on the east bank of the Meuse captured and held.

17 August. Further positions lost to French attack east of Bixschoote.

18 August. Meuse east bank trenches lost to French counterattack.

19 August. British tanks capture pillboxes near St. Julien but these are retaken briefly after a successful counterattack. Fifth Army evacuates Talou Ridge and other positions prior to French attacks scheduled for 20 August.

20 August. General Kohl reports that seventeen divisions are 'verbraucht' (used up) as a result of the Ypres offensive. Defences north of Verdun pushed back a depth of 1½ miles on an eleven-mile front with 5000 POWs taken by the French; positions lost include Avocourt Wood, Hill 240 and Mort Homme.

21 August. Near Verdun the villages of Côte de l'Oie, Regnéville and Samogneux are lost to a French attack and, in the north near Lens, territory lost to a Canadian attack.

22 August. Heavy losses inflicted upon attacking British forces at St. Julien and along the Menin road; small territorial losses to the British including Glencorse Wood.

24 August. Camard Wood and Hill 304 lost during French attacks on a 2000 yard front that penetrate lines to a distance of 1½ miles.

25 August. Territory yielded to attacking French troops north of Hill 304 near Verdun; losses on this front since 20 August include over 9000 POWs, over sixty guns, machine guns and mortars. On the Ypres front the British losses are over 68,000 since offensive started.

26 August. French troops reach the outskirts of Beaumont near the east bank of the Meuse and repulse counterattack. Around Ypres, mud assists containment of British advance to 2000 yards. On the Somme, British forces take and hold half a mile of trenches east of Hargicourt, near St.Quentin.

28 August. Troops almost back to start positions before the Verdun offensive started.

30 August. Light raid on British trenches southeast of Lens repulsed.

31 August. Menin road ridge defences lightly shelled by British artillery and some British advance posts taken north of the St. Julien-Poelcapelle road. Near Hubertise on the Aisne Front some territory is taken by a French attack.

1 September. British positions at Havrincourt near Cambrai are captured and occupied before British counterattack push troops back. Four counterattacks northeast of Craonne against French positions fail.

2 September. Attacks against British advanced outposts near Havrincourt fail.

3 September. French raid positions on the Souain-Somme Py road to find poison gas storage site. Small amount of territory yielded to British attack near St. Julien.

4 September. Air raid on British base (hospital) kills four Americans.

5 September. Shellfire kills two US soldiers repairing the railway near Gouzeacourt.

6 September. British troops pushed back near Frezenberg.

8 September. French capture the villages of Caurières, Chaume and Fosses on the Verdun Front along with 800 POWs.

9 September. 600 yards of trenches at Villeret and 400 yards northwest of St. Quentin lost to British troops. Counterattack against French positions on the east bank of the Meuse repulsed.

13 September. Raid at Langemarck repulsed by British troops. French forward positions north of Caurière Wood successfully counterattacked.

14 September. French recapture positions north of Caurière Wood.

15 September. Attack on Portuguese troops at Neuve Chapelle repulsed and strongpoint north of Inverness Copse lost to British attack.

16 September. Attack on Apremont Forest near St. Mihiel repulsed by French.

20 September. British attack against Passchendaele-Gheluvelt line after eight-hour creeping barrage, taking Glencorse Wood, Hollebeke, Inverness Copse, part of Polygon Wood and Veldhoek, despite eleven counterattacks.

21 September. Attacks on British positions on Tower Hamlets ridge repulsed; over the two days of fighting more than 3,000 men lost as POWs but more than 20,000 casualties inflicted on the British.

24 September. Near Verdun the French repulse attacks north of Bezonvaux, Chaume Woods and Fosses.

25 September. Troops penetrate between Polygon Wood and Tower Hamlets but later retire under pressure from British troops.

26 September. Very heavy fighting as British and Anzac troops with tanks assault Polygon Wood; four counterattacks made using eingreif (intervention) divisions resulting in heavy casualties, including 1600 POWs.

27 September. Last part of Polygon Wood falls to Australian troops and all counterattack made east of Ypres are repulsed by British troops.

29 September. First tank unit formed.

30 September. Three flamethrower attacks against British positions between Polygon Wood and Tower hamlets unsuccessful; over 5000 POWs and eleven guns lost to the British. In the Alsace region troops take and hold French positions at Berry-au-Bac briefly.

1 October. Counterattack against British forces in the Ypres Salient fails, but attack on French positions between Bezonvaux and Chaume Wood successful. Army strength on the Western Front now stands at 147 divisions with 12,432 guns.

2 October. Further counterattack against British forces in the Ypres Salient fails, but assault on French trenches near Beaumont gains a foothold. Repeated French counterattacks between Hill 344 and Samogneux unsuccessful.

3 October. Counterattack against British forces in the Ypres Salient fails, as does a French counterattack between Hill 344 and Samogneux. Troops massing for attacks east of Reims hit by French artillery.

4 October. Using tanks, British troops take Broodseinde Ridge and the village of Capelle; troops fall back on average 700 yards on a twelve-mile front. Crest of Ypres Ridge reached by British forces. As a result of the high casualty rate, Ludendorff recommends forming an advanced zone of mobile troops in no-mans-land to slow down attacking infantry in order to provide easier targets for the artillery. counterattack against British forces in the Ypres Salient fails.

5 October. Further counterattack against British forces in the Ypres Salient fails; over 4000 POWs taken by the British during the counterattacks. In the sixty-seven days since the British offensive began thirty-six miles of territory have been lost along with fifty-five guns and over 20,000 POWs; losses inflicted upon the British forces are nearly 163,000.

6 October. British repulse dusk attack on Polygon Wood taking 380 POWs. At Verdun, French trenches at Hill 344 taken for a short time.

7 October. British troops attacked at Reutel on the Ypres Front. Big raid on French positions in the Champagne region repulsed, as is the attack near Craonne. Start of a month-long series of eventually successful localised attacks by the French to take the Chemin des Dames road.

8 October. French forces launch an attack southwest of Beaumont in the Champagne region.

9 October. After severe fighting on a six-mile front, British troops gain the crest of Broodseinde Ridge and reach the south edge of Houthulst Forest taking 2000 POWs for a loss of 7000 casualties. A counterattack is launched against British positions on a 2000 yard front south of the Ypres-Staden railway line. On the Verdun front, north of Chaume Wood, after an artillery duel, the first line of French trenches is penetrated.

Ludendorff and the General Staff at his headquarters.

Feeding the troops was an essential in maintaining morale – the *gulaschkanone* (goulash cannon) or *hungerabwehrkanone* (hunger defence cannon) – to the British, a field cooker.

Hungerabwehrkanon

10 October. Troops pull back along the Corverbeck valley as a result of French attacks.

11 October. Brief penetration of French advanced positions on Hill 344 and to the north. In Flanders, counterattack to the east of Dreibank is repulsed by the French First Army. As a result of the continued losses on the Flanders Front, Crown Prince Rupprecht suggests a tactical withdrawal to economise on men and materiel.

12 October. Heavy fighting in poor conditions, mud and rain, on six-mile front northeast of Ypres at Passchendaele. Twelve Eastern Front divisions scheduled for the Italian Front are re-routed to Flanders to replace losses.

15 October. 90,000 rounds of Phosgene gas fired at French troops in the Ailette Basin near Laffaux on the Aisne Front.

16 October. French begin bombardment prior to a limited offensive on the Aisne front but their attack west of Craonne is successfully stopped.

18 October. Attack on Vauclere Plateau, west of Craonne, held by French troops.

21 October. First US troops enter the line at Lunéville in the Lorraine Front.

22 October. Anglo-French advance on a $2^1/2$ mile front on the Ypres-Staden railway line; south end of Houthulst Forest lost with 200 POWs.

23 October. Part of Houthulst Forest retaken. Proposals for a spring offensive submitted. Temporary foothold gained northeast of Hill 344. French take three villages and Fort Malmaison along with 8,000 POWs and 70 guns in a two mile advance; one division heavily gassed and routed. French pressure forces withdrawal behind the Oise-Aisne Canal.

25 October. French pressure on positions near the River Ailette and the Oise Canal result in the loss, over two days, of 11,157 POWs, more than 400 guns and mortars, plus 720 machine guns, for the loss of 12,000 French casualties.

26 October. The French thrust against Houthulst Forest and the Canadian attack against Poelcapelle result in some territorial loss around Bercelaere, Gheluvelt, Passchendaele and Zandvorde.

27 October. Belgian and French troops push through the lines on the Ypres-Dixmunde road to a depth of up to $1^1/2$ miles.

28 October. Fighting on the Oise Canal and an advance is made against French positions at Chaume Wood and Bezonvaux.

30 October. Canadian troops pushed back to the outskirts of Passchendaele after five counterattacks.

1 November. Seventh Army is forced to retire from Chemin des Dames when outflanked by French troops.

3 November. Trench raiders kill three, and capture eleven, US soldiers.

6 November. Passchendaele lost to early morning Canadian attack. Goudberg and Mosselmarkt also lost with 464 POWs. French forces take Merckem.

7 November. French positions at Chaume Wood successfully attacked.

8 November. British troops succeed in raiding trenches near Armentières and Fresnoy. Bolshevik Revolution starts in Russia.

10 November. French assault at Chaume Wood successfully regains the positions lost on 7 November. Three counterattacks hold Canadian attack to a 500-yard advance north along the main ridge east of the Passchendaele-Westroosebeke road, and inflict nearly 1200 casualties.

11 November. Ludendorff proposes spring offensive at Mons conference. Raid on French positions at Hartmannsweilerkopf.

13 November. Infantry assault in the Ypres Salient fails.

14 November. British positions north of the Menin road and northeast of Passchendaele attacked.

17 November. Positions in Flanders, on the Somme and in the Champagne region raided by British and French troops.

18 November. Trench raids on British positions northwest of St. Quentin.

19 November. British trenches raided in parts of the Flanders Sector.

20 November. Nineteen British divisions and 389 tanks assault positions around Cambrai without preliminary bombardment; tanks flatten wire and rout front line infantry resulting in a breach six miles wide and up to 4000 yards deep. Attackers lose 4000 casualties but capture 4200 POWs, 123 guns and 281 machine guns. Unteroffizier Krüger's gun knocks out seven tanks. To improve defence capability in the St Quentin area, the crossings over the canal are blown up.

21 November. Using tanks, the British take Cantaing with 300 POWs as well as Fontaine-Notre-Dame and Tadpole Copse. Counterattack by *20 Division* recaptures Moeuvres on the northern flank of the British attack. Counterattack beaten off after French storm Craonne Plateau salient.

22 November. Counterattack recaptures Fontaine-Notre-Dame from British troops.

23 November. Sixteen of the attacking tanks destroyed (five by flak guns) during the British attack on Bourlon Wood and village; attacking troops stopped from reaching the village.

24 November. Defenders on Bourlon Hill repel British attack but fall back in the village and lose Fontaine-Notre-Dame.

25 November. Counterattack on British positions at Bourlon. French attack in Samogneux sector takes 800 POWs.

26 November. Seven divisions now involved in defence of Cambrai Sector.

27 November. British Guards Division pushed back in Bourlon and Fontaine Sectors. Twenty new divisions sent to defend Cambrai Sector and prepare a counterattack.

28 November. British positions in Bourlon Wood bombarded with 16,000 gas and high explosives.

29 November. West of Bourlon Wood troops pushed back by British attacks.

30 November. Employing infiltration tactics and close air support, eleven divisions attack on a twelve-mile front, pushing through to La Vacquerie and Gouzeaucourt, capturing 6000 POWs and 158 guns, although latter village later retaken by British Guards Division. British attacks since 31 July had caused around 400,000 casualties but transfer of over 500,000 from Eastern Front and elsewhere begins.

1 December. Gonnelieu lost, but British troops pushed from Masnières salient; continued heavy fighting for Bourlon Wood. Attacks against French positions in the Verdun area are unsuccessful.

2 December. Heavy fighting for the high ground above La Vacquerie.

3 December. British attacks result in the loss of the southwest corner of Polygon Wood but they withdraw from La Vacquerie and bridgehead over canal east of Marcoing.

4 December. Threat of further attacks causes British troops to evacuate Cambrai Salient.

6 December. Further attacks made around La Vacquerie.

7 December. British troops now up to 2½ miles in advance of Cambrai start lines in the north, but have fallen back an equal amount in the south.

8 December. Over two hundred trench raids against British positions result in sixty-two enemy units being identified.

10 December. Attack on Chaume Wood repulsed by French forces while British capture post east of Boursies on the Bapaume-Cambrai road.

12 December. British forces pushed out from small salient between Bullecourt and Quéant.

13 December. Skirmishing on the Flanders and Verdun Fronts and at Cambrai.

14 December. Part of British front line trench captured near Polderhoek Château in Flanders.

15 December. Snow hampers any offensive operations.

16 December. Troops retire under pressure from British troops east of Avion.

17 December. Fighting near the Ypres-Comines Canal.

20 December. Fog assists capture of British advanced post west of Messines.

21 December. French hold lines after fierce fighting at Hartmannswillerkopf.

22 December. Some British advanced posts stormed on the Ypres-Staden railway line.

26 December. French resist attacks in Caurières wood.

27 December. General Hutier from the Eastern Front takes over the new Eighteenth Army at St. Quentin.

28 December. Parts of Welsh Ridge lost to British attack; counterattacks repulsed.

31 December. Over 180,000 US troops now in Europe.

A trench complex near Boiry.

Kiesgrube bei Boiry

Clearing deep dugouts after the rain.

A year earlier – now only a memory, a well-provisioned soldiers' canteen. The motto reads, 'In words and works everytime good German'.

A British tank destroyed in the Arras offensive.

With mobile warfare, comfortable underground billets also became a thing of the past – an officer's billet in 1915.

Sports competitions were a popular way of resting troops and improving unit morale.

On the Western Front every soldier suffered from lice – a mobile delousing station and its customers.

Out of the line an ordinary soldier's life could be had between the training and fatigues.

Wechselstube. Bureau de Change.

When the Germans pulled back to previously prepared positions in early 1917, they left behind traces of their temporary tenure.

Out at rest – a meal consisting of Kaiserbrot and ersatz coffee.

A trench machine gun in use as an anti-aircraft weapon.

The main road through Varennes in May 1917.

A celebration on the Arras front on 30 April 1917.

To help bolster the Turkish Army, Germany sent thousands of troops to the Middle East. This picture was taken in Palestine at the end of 1917. The Star worn by the two soldiers on the right, is a Turkish award.

Like Britain, Germany also had troops fighting in distant parts of the world – soldiers in Africa.

There was still considerable fighting on the Eastern front. Here troops are being ferried across the River Daugava to assault the city of Riga – the last battle on the Eastern front. The cessation of hostilities gave Ludendorff the troops he needed for the coming attacks on the Western front.

Gas mask drill was an essential part of training.

No matter what the situation, the paperwork had to be completed.

To accommodate the ever-increasing numbers of troops garrisoned behind the lines any available building was taken over. In this case, the School of Arts, Industry and Commerce was converted into a barracks.

Stoutly constructed trenches opposite French positions in a wooded area.

While the Western Front was the most important battle area, the Eastern Front also needed hundreds of thousands of men. Here cavalry cross a river in Rumania in 1917.

A Kaiserparade near Hinzenburg on 6 September 1917 for troops defending the German border.

Although technically enemies, this picture suggests otherwise.

September 1917 – the arrival of mail was an important morale booster. Note the pristine condition of the trenches suggesting a quiet backwater of the war.

A divisional parade during May 1917; another method of keeping up morale.

Landwehr troops on the Eastern Front in early 1917. A year later, the best and fittest of them would be serving on the Western Front.

German POWs captured during the Arras offensive in temporary accommodation.

A strange card to send home – a cemetery with the by-line 'Greetings from the West'.

Rear defence positions ready for occupation should the need arise.

The first American POWs were captured after hard fighting. Here they are presented for the public (note their size in comparision to their captors).

As in the previous years, life behind the front was clean and orderly – the main street of the village with the village commander's office on the right.

A disguised anti-aircraft battery made up of standard field guns.

Comfortable billets far behind the lines.

A tank from 8 Battalion Tank Corps captured at Cambrai, used in the War funds drive in Leipzig.

An officers' celebration during August 1917 – note the wall mural.

Soldiers being decorated for their valour during autumn 1917.

Cookhouse duty some distance behind the lines was preferable to life in the front line.

Millions of Americans were in training and ready to fight when they arrived in France. Here a unit practises marching before being shipped to France.

Verdun was an important battle area in 1916 and continued to be so for the rest of the war. This is the view from Hill 304 in the Verdun area in 1918.

Chronology of the Western Front
1917-1918

1918

1 January. Flamethrower attack southeast of Verdun successful, but raids in vicinity of Beaumont and Chaume Wood repulsed by French.

2 January. British repulse trench raid near La Bassée.

3 January. Troops south of Lens pull back under pressure from British attacks, while in Alsace attack near Anspach repulsed by the French.

4 January. Four British outposts near the Canal du Nord withdraw under pressure.

5 January. Raids east of Cambrai and near Ypres repulsed.

8 January. French Foreign Legion takes 188 POWs, sixteen machineguns and nine mortars during a trench raid in the Meuse sector.

9 January. Canadians raid positions south of Lens.

10 January. Raid on trenches in the Ypres sector by British; French troops in the St. Quentin area relieved by the British.

11 January. Front lines raided by French troops in the Argonne, Champagne and Vosges.

12 January. Four trench raids on British positions south of Lens and east of Monchy fail.

14 January. British raid positions north of Lens.

21 January. Spring offensive decision taken.

22 January. British trenches east of Loos and near La Bassée and St. Quentin raided.

23 January. French trenches taken east of Nieuport but lost to a counterattack. Further east French raid in the Champagne region is beaten off.

24 January. French trenches at Cauriéres Wood, near Verdun and also north of the Aisne raided unsuccessfully.

28 January. Limited French attacks in Champagne and Alsace.

1 February. Seventeenth Army formed in Artois region. Captain Bomschlegel restores thirty captured British tanks ready for combat use.

4 February. Nineteenth Army formed in Lorraine under Count Bothmer.

8 February. Trench raids against French positions on the Aisne and Meuse Fronts.

10 February. Thirty-three POWs taken by Australian troops during trench raid at Warneton.

12 February. Trenches near Hagnicourt-Lens raided by Canadian forces.

13 February. Troops in the Tahure-Butte du Mesnil Salient pushed back. In the attacks French take 177 POWs.

18 February. Trenches in Houthulst Forest raided by British forces.

20 February. Over 500 POWs taken by French during a large raid on positions east of Nancy.

22 February. British positions raided on the Ypres-Staden line.

23 February. American and French troops raid positions over the River Ailette.

28 February. Western Front strength now 180 divisions.

1 March. Portuguese trenches near Neuve Chapelle raided and held. French pushed back slightly at the Butte du Mesnil.

3 March. British positions raided in Flanders and on the Somme.

4 March. Raid on Aloof Trench west of Lens fails.

5 March. New cipher introduced prior to offensive. Positions north of Pervyse attacked by Belgian troops.

Landwehr troops in Russia enjoying the calm of a snowy day. Within a year the best of them would be on the Western Front.

A machine gunner poses for the family back home – note the metal badge on the right arm.

The Allied air-forces brought the war home to the German population by night attacks on selected cities. By World War 2 standards the damage done was more psychological than physically destructive.

6 March. Night raid on Belgian positions near Ramscapelle repulsed.

9 March. Trenches near Neuve Chapelle lost to Portuguese counterattack. British and French positions between Ypres and St. Quentin bombarded with 500,000 Mustard and Phosgene gas shells.

10 March. Diversionary operations around Verdun and in the Champagne area prior to real offensive; Operation Michael ordered by Hindenburg.

12 March. French positions at Vaudesincourt, (east of Reims) attacked.

13 March. Strongpoint southeast of Polygon Wood lost to British attack.

14 March. Troops on the Butte du Mesnil pushed back by French counterattack.

16 March. Most artillery in position for offensive and infantry begin night approach marches. French raid on trenches near Verdun takes 160 POWs while similar raid against French positions takes 200 POWs.

18 March. Heavy local attacks on Belgian positions on the Yser Front fail.

19 March. Troops issued with special gas mask filters, twenty anti-tank bullets and grenades ready for start of offensive. Near St. Quentin, troops bombarded by the British with eighty-five tons of Phosgene, causing over 1000 casualties. French positions on the Meuse and in Champagne attacked.

20 March. 190 divisions now available on the Western Front.

21 March. Operation Michael – British Fifth Army attacked on forty-two mile front and British Third Army on a forty-three mile front. Stormtroops attack in dense mist and advance up to 4$^{1}/_{2}$ miles against fierce resistance; attack assisted by tanks. Advancing troops take 21,000 POWs, over 500 guns, forty-six villages and more territory than was lost on the Somme in the July – December 1916 offensive. In the Artois region British fire fifty-seven tons of Phosgene shells on positions near Lens. Hand-to-hand fighting during attacks on French positions between Maisons de Champagne and Navarin. American 42nd Division shelled with Mustard gas.

22 March. Attack continues, pushing British troops further back, taking another 16,000 POWs and 200 guns; Epéhy and Roisel captured and Crozat Canal crossed.

23 March. Troops take Ham and Péronne. British abandon Flesquières Salient. Paris shelled by 8.26 inch guns at range of twenty-four miles, killing 256 and injuring 620.

24 March. Enemy pushed back and troops cross the Somme between Ham and Péronne and further south capture Chauny rail junction. British cavalry attack at Villeselve captures three machine guns.

25 March. Bapaume (British counterattack beaten off), Nesle and Noyon captured. British Fifth Army pushed back about four miles on a twenty-three mile front; enemy front now fractured.

26 March. 3 Marine and 54 Reserve Divisions take Albert and Roye from the French. British light tanks halt advance in Colincamps-Hébuterne area.

27 March. Troops enter Montdidier; capture Proyart, Morcourt and Lamotte-Warfuseé with ten mile gap between enemy armies. British hold up advance to the Somme and Amiens at Rosières.

28 March. Operation Mars against British troops around Arras fails but attacks towards Amiens gain three miles. Démuin, Hamel and Mézières captured but retreating British troops not cut off; three villages recaptured by French troops.

29 March. Enemy driven back on a seven mile front between the Avre and Luce but overall offensive starts to slacken.

30 March. Enemy recapture Moreuil Wood but further south French troops fall back on a twenty-five mile front, losing six villages.

30 March. Since the start of the offensive 75,000 POWs taken and about 1,000 guns. Moreuil Wood retaken from British troops. Hangard captured by British but regained by counterattack.

31 March. Troops withdraw slightly between Montdidier and Lassigny under French pressure.

1 April. Heavy but inconclusive fighting at Albert, Grivesnes and Hébuterne. Rifle Wood lost to British attack along with 100 POWs and thirteen machineguns.

2 April. Ayette lost to British troops.

4 April. French counterattack gains ground in Castel-Cantigny sector and Australians repulse attack in front of Villers-Brettoneux. Since the start of the offensive, 1200 sq. miles of territory taken with 1300 guns and 90,000 POWs.

5 April. *50 Prussian Reserve Division* advances nearly a mile on the Ancre Front but British counterattack near Hébuterne takes 200 POWs.

6 April. Further severe inconclusive fighting around Albert and Hébuterne. Seventh Army drives French Sixth Army from bridgehead north of Ailette River taking 2300 POWs. Beaumont, in the Meuse Sector, attacked.

7 April. Attacks on British positions at Bucquoy repulsed.

8 April. Whole British front shelled with 40,000 Mustard gas shells on Armentières. On the Aisne, Coucy le Château re-occupied and the Oise-Aisne canal line reached.

9 April. Operation Georgette offensive against British First and Second Armies begins on a ten-mile front. Portuguese 2 Division falls back losing 6000 POWs, creating a gap for advancing troops, but British 55 Division on southern flank resists, taking 750 POWs and 100 machine guns. Lys sector bombarded with 2000 tons of diphenylchlorarsine, Mustard gas and Phosgene. Attack on Hengard successful but later lost to French counterattack.

10 April. An eight-division attack on a six-mile front pushes British out of Armentières but fails to take the Lys Line of defences. Messines Ridge recaptured.

11 April. Troops enter Armentières and take Merville and Hill 63. Number of POWs taken is now over 20,000.

12 April. Attacks in Apremont Forest in the Argonne repulsed by American and French troops. Offensive slows down in front of Hazebrouck as enemy resistance stiffens.

13 April. Troops only push British forces back 800 yards in front of Bailleul. Commander of II Bavarian Corps sacked.

14 April. A field gun destroys six British machine guns, but all attacks in Flanders fail.

15 April. Bailleul and Wulverghem captured by the Alpenkorps and two other divisions. British troops start to pull back on Passchendaele Ridge.

16 April. Passchendaele taken along with Wytschaete and Meteren (1000 New Zealand POWs captured); latter two towns lost to British counterattacks.

17 April. Wytschaete and Meteren captured. Heavy Mustard gas attack on Villers-Bretonneux. Belgian forces capture forty-two machine guns and 700 POWs during an attack northwest of Dixmunde.

18 April. Using tank support, French troops advance 500 yards near Castel southeast of Amiens, taking 650 POWs. British positions between Givenchy and the Lys heavily attacked and territory gained.

19 April. Enemy lines between Kemmel and Ypres bombarded with 2000 tons of diphenylchlorarsine, Mustard and Phosgene gas. After initial success at Seicheprey the Americans and French counterattack regains the lost territory.

23 April. Heavy attacks against British positions at Albert and between the Somme and the Avre.

24 April. Villers-Bretonneux taken, along with nearly 400 POWs, by two divisions and thirteen tanks. A7V tank 'Elfreide' knocked out after disabling two British machine gun tanks in the first tank battle. Night counter-attack by enemy troops retakes Villers-Bretonneux.

25 April. French troops pushed off Kemmel Hill by seven divisions in five hours.

26 April. Attacks at Voormezeele repulsed but Lochre taken from the French temporarily. Hangard Wood lost to French attacks. All counterattacks fail.

28 April. Raid at Langemarck repulsed by Belgians.

29 April. A thirteen-division attack on a ten-mile front in Flanders achieves only minor gains and the offensive is suspended.

30 April. Operation Georgette halted.

1 May. Raid south of Mount Kemmel repulsed and troops pushed back near Lochre by the French. There are now 204 divisions on the western Front.

2 May. Hill 82 and woodland south of Hailles in the Avre Valley lost after French attack.

3 May. American lines opposite Cantigny bombarded with fifteen tons of Mustard gas.

4 May. Enemy lines in Locre and south of Ypres heavily shelled.

5 May. British advance at Morlancourt in the Somme Region.

6 May. French positions raided south of Locre.

9 May. La Cyette-Voormezeele sector attacked without success. On the Somme Front, some territory is yielded to French troops attacking at Grivesnes, northwest of Montdidier.

10 May. Front line trench northwest of Albert lost to British attack. French positions in the Argonne and Lorraine bombarded with gas. American positions in the St. Mihiel-Toul sector also shelled with gas.

13 May. Italian troops move into the line west of Verdun.

14 May. Attack on a mile front southwest of Morlancourt successful but ground lost to enemy counterattack.

15 May. Using 1800 trains, twenty-eight assault divisions begin concentrating opposite Chemin des Dames.

16 May. British raid trenches near Beaumont Hamel.

18 May. Ville-sur-Ancre raid and 360 POWs lost during night attack to Entente forces.

19 May. French take 400 POWs during attack at Kemmel.

21 May. British raid trenches near Arras.

24 May. British positions in Nieppe Forest shelled with gas. Tank attack on French Bardonelles trench fails because tanks cannot cross the trench.

25 May. Artillery bombardment of Villers-Bretonneux.

27 May. After a 4000 gun bombardment on a twenty-four mile front on the Aisne, twenty-five divisions capture Chemin des Dames and Craonne and advance twelve miles. Long-range bombardment of Paris recommences.

28 May. Aisne bridgehead now forty miles wide and fifteen miles deep with troops across the River Vesle. Machine gunner kills General des Vallières, commander of the French 151 Division. Troops' behaviour deteriorates due to drunkenness. On the Somme Front, Cantigny is lost to American troops who beat off all counterattacks.

29 May. On the Marne Sector advancing troops capture Fère-en-Tardenois, Soissons, the Vregny plateau, heights south of the River Vesle and cross the River Ourcq, pushing the French out of the 'Paris Line'. However, attacks against positions near Mount Kemmel falter.

30 May. Marne offensive continues with the capture of Château-Thiery and Dormans. French retire from the River Ailette.

31 May. French light tanks halt the advance in Retz Forest.

1 June. Troops attacking between the Oise and the Marne held by American troops, but eventually reach outskirts of Villers-Cotterêts Forest, forty miles away from Paris. Between 1000 and 2000 cases of flu reported per division.

2 June. Faverelles lost to French troops during a counterattack between the rivers Ourcq and Marne.

3 June. French retake Choisy Hill during fierce fighting between Soissons and Noyon. After reaching the Marne, American troops halt the advance at Château-Thiery. One hundred POWs captured when Franco-American forces take the bridgehead at Jaulogne.

4 June. Attack at Veuilly Wood halted by American soldiers.

6 June. Bouresches, Bouresches Wood and Vaux counterattacked by American troops; Veuilly-La-Poterie and Vinly lost to joint American-French attack and Fligny recaptured by the British.

8 June. Raid on Canadian trenches near Neuville-Vitasse repelled by Lewis gunner.

9 June. Operation Gneisenau starts with midnight barrage and an attack three hours later with eleven divisions between Montdidier and Noyon; takes 8000 POWs and advances six miles.

10 June. Troops advance a further two miles.

11 June. Enemy counterattack with tanks and air support takes three villages, nineteen guns and 1000 POWs but attack blunted by stiffening resistance. On the Somme enemy troops capture 300 POWs during a peaceful penetration.

12 June. A five-division attack west of Soissons gains little against French troops with tanks; whole operation called off. French attacks between Montdidier and Noyon gain over 3000 yards.

14 June. French bombard trenches in the Matz area with Mustard gas. Trenches along La Bassée Canal raided by British troops.

18 June. French block attack between Sillery and Trigny.

22 June. Enemy tanks and infantry raid trenches at Bucquoy.

25 June. Belleau Wood lost to American troops after twenty days of fighting.

28 June. Three villages and 1200 POWs lost to Franco-American counterattacks on the edge of Villers-Cotterêts Forest. In Flanders, British raid at La Becque results in the front line being pushed back by a mile on a three mile front, losing 440 POWs. French troops recapture a hill near Treloup on the Marne.

30 June. Total casualties since 21 March nearly 900,000.

1 July. On the Marne Front, Vaux taken by American units.

2 July. French attacks near Moulin-sous-Touvent take some ground and 1000 POWs.

4 July. British and American units advance on a 3 1/2 mile front to a depth of 1 1/2 miles capturing Hamel, two guns, 171 machine guns, two mortars and 1472 POWs. Northeast of Villers-Bretonneux troops pushed back 2000 yards.

7 July. Two Austrian divisions arrive on the Western Front. Some ground lost north and south of the River Somme.

8 July. On the Aisne, French troops advance east of Villers-Cotterêts, taking 346 POWs.

10 July. Courcy, north of the River Ourcq, is lost to French attacks.

11 July. French deserter betrays imminent enemy offensive on the Marne. Influenza epidemic so severe that Crown Prince Rupprecht considers calling off Operation Hagen.

12 July. Castel-Auchin Farm captured by the French. Fifth offensive postponed.

14 July. American positions in Champagne and the Meuse regions shelled with Mustard and Phosgene gas.

15 July. Operation Friedensturm launched against enemy east of Reims to the Marne, with forty-three divisions on a fifty mile front after a four-hour barrage. Rapid advance to the Marne at Fossoy against French troops. East of Reims offensive fails, with all tanks knocked out by French guns. To the west of Reims, Italian troops holding the line pushed back. Two divisions attempting to force a Marne crossing held up by a US Infantry regiment. Eight divisions achieve a nine-mile wide, thirteen-mile deep bridgehead at Dormans. Paris shelled by long-range gun.

16 July. Advance checked east of Reims but moves forward slowly to Prunay. To the west of Reims, troops advance along the Marne to Renil threatening Epernay; forces north of St. Agnan La Chapelle counter-attacked by US units.

17 July. Advance on Epernay continues, capturing Montasin, later lost to French counterattack. Italian counter-attack pushes troops back from Nanteuil-Pourcy. South of Prunay, advancing French troops recapture lost ground.

18 July. Franco-American attack on a twenty seven mile front between Belleau and Fonteroy taking 12000 POWs, 250 guns and advancing 4 1/2 miles towards Soissons in the north and between three and five miles in the south. Two divisions sent to the attacked front but fourteen divisions south of the Marne ordered to retire. Artillery transfer to Flanders is cancelled, as is attack in the Reims area. Counterattack at Prunay pushes French back and village is captured.

19 July. Defenders overrun by British attack at Meteren in Flanders losing 300 POWs. Continued Franco-American attacks in the Champagne-Marne area push troops back two miles towards Soissons-Château-Thiery road, taking 3000 POWs and 150 guns; road successfully retaken by 20 Division. South of the Marne, Montoisin lost to enemy advance.

20 July. Troops pull back across the Marne; total losses in the area since the enemy offensive started are 20000 POWs and 400 guns. Hidden machine guns slow down British advance in the Tardenois area but 500 POWs lost and troops fall back a mile.

21 July. Five-mile night withdrawal in Château-Thiery area; town taken by advancing French troops. In the Ardre valley, counterattack takes Coutrim and Marfaux from the enemy.

22 July. Further stabilisation of the front five miles back from Château-Thiery between the rivers Ourcq and Marne. Southern half of the salient abandoned.

Lille was a garrison town with facilities to cater for large numbers of troops.

A Home Front card asking that gold be exchanged for iron to help the war effort.

SPA – the villa that housed the German HQ (Château Neubois) and was later occupied by the Allied Mission.

Max Herrndobler, a thirty-seven year old soldier killed the day before the great offensive.

Zum frommen Andenken
im Gebete
an den ehrengeachteten Herrn
Max Herrndobler
Gütler von Johanniskirchen
Soldat bei einem bayer. Inft.-Regt.
4. Kompagnie

POSTKARTE

GOLD GAB ICH ZUR WEHR
EISEN NAHM ICH ZUR EHR

BRINGT EUREN
GOLDSCHMUCK
DEN GOLDANKAUFS-
STELLEN

23 July. Against stiffening resistance, French advance on a two-mile front north of the River Ourcq, reaching Faux. Marfaux lost to British counterattack. On the Somme front, enemy attacks push troops back two miles on a four-mile front towards the Avre valley between Moreuil and Sauvillers capturing three villages, five guns, 275 machine guns and 1858 POWs.

24 July. Eighteen divisions in the Champagne/Marne battle zone not battle-worthy. Further enemy advances along the Marne in Fère Forest and north of Château-Thiery towards Fère-en-Tardenois.

25 July. Fère Forest occupied as enemy troops advance two miles capturing La Croise Range, Oulchy-le-Château and Villemontoire. Troops told to retire to the Fère-en-Tardenois line on the night of 27 July.

26 July. General retreat towards Eperrau is extended to Marne and Ourcq valleys.

27 July. Retreating troops pursued by enemy cavalry and tanks.

28 July. Since 26 July, enemy forces have advanced four miles on a twenty-mile front.

29 July. Kaiser allows retreat to the Blücher position north of Vesle. Fierce resistance between Fère-en-Tardenois and St. Euphrasie allows troops to escape French encirclement. On the Somme, enemy advance on a two-mile front at Morlancourt taking thirty-six machine guns and 138 POWs.

30 July. Ludendorff orders withdrawal to Blücher position. In the Champagne/Marne sector, fierce resistance slows the enemy advance but Romigny-St.Gemme falls.

31 July. 1919 class of recruits almost used up as reinforcements. In the Neuilly sector on the Meuse, French positions bombarded with 340,000 gas shells. Severe fighting around Seringes on the Champagne/Marne Front.

1 August. During the night, the retirement to Vesle begins after further enemy advances north of the Ourcq net 700 POWs. Number of companies reduced from four to three in 400 strong battalions. Troops regroup behind the rivers Aisne and Vesle.

2 August. French troops reoccupy Soissons and fifty villages in their six-mile advance. Troops regroup behind the rivers Aisne and Vesle.

3 August. On the Somme, troops withdraw behind the Ancre. Enemy continue their advance on a thirty-mile front, eventually taking Fismes.

4 August. Since 18 July 700 guns and 35000 POWs lost on the Marne/Aisne Front. Rearguard troops withdraw to north bank of the River Vesle. Withdrawal in the Somme Sector on a ten-mile front between Montdidier and Moreuil on the east bank of the River Avre.

5 August. Paris bombarded by long-range gun.

6 August. On the Somme a divisional counterattack at Morlancourt regains much ground and takes 250 British POWs, while on the Marne/Aisne Front the enemy reach the River Vesle. Army Group Boehn formed and General Carlowitz takes over Ninth Army.

8 August. The black day of the German Army in this war – enemy attack on the Somme, taking nearly 900 guns and over 29,000 POWs.

9 August. Enemy advance on the Somme continues but at a slower pace. British advance west of Merville towards Locon.

10 August. Montdidier garrison surrounded and captured by French Army during seven-mile advance. Further south French assault pushes defenders up to four miles back on the Oise front.

11 August. Counterattacks stabilising the Amiens front.

12 August. Seventh Army now commanded by Eberhardt while Boehn (previous commander) forms new Army Group from *Second, Ninth* and *Eighteenth* Armies whose commanders are relieved of their command by the Kaiser.

14 August. Decision taken to evacuate the Ancre Sector. Ludendorff recommends immediate peace negotiations.

15 August. Counterattack around Damery on the Somme repulsed. French troops take the Lassigny Massif and the town.

16 August. Troops pushed back in Roye Sector by enemy attack.

17 August. Two thousand yards lost to French attack between the Oise and Aisne rivers as well as over 2000 POWs.

18 August. British advance between Vieux Berquin and Bailleul takes nearly 700 POWs. Positions at Mervillor near Baccarat bombarded with twelve tons of Phosgene. In Flanders, Outtersteene and Hoegenacker Ridges and Merville lost to British attack.

19 August. Le Hamel on the Aisne lost to French forces.

20 August. French attack between the rivers Aisne and Oise takes 8000 POWs and advances three miles; attacks repulsed north of Soissons. Since the start of the enemy offensive on the Somme twenty-seven villages and sixty-five square miles of territory have been lost, as well as over 9000 POWs, nearly 200 guns and over 1000 machine guns and mortars.

21 August. Enemy attack on a ten mile front at Albert, using tanks, aircraft and smoke, pushes defenders back between two and three miles for the loss of 2000 POWs; counterattack repulsed by the enemy.

22 August. Albert lost and counterattacks repulsed.

23 August. Enemy attack on thirty-three mile front on the Somme, taking 7000 POWs, and in some areas pushes the defenders back up to two miles. Further enemy attacks at night.

24 August. In Flanders the enemy capture Givenchy Craters; on the Somme Thiepval Ridge and Mory Copse are lost to a British attack.

25 August. Further enemy advance on the Somme takes Mametz Wood and two villages north of Bapaume.

26 August. Army Group Commanders ask for permission to withdraw seventy miles to the Antwerp-Meuse position; Ludendorff allows a ten-mile withdrawal on a fifty-five mile front during the night. Enemy attack south of Arras captures Monchy-le-Preux and advances four miles.

27 August. Greenland Hill and Delville and Trônes Woods captured by British troops. French recapture Chauny and Roye.

28 August. In the Artois region, troops have been pushed back up to five miles with the loss of 3300 POWs but *2 Bavarian Corps* hold on to Fresnes-Rouvroy line; general retirement from the Scarpe to above the River Aisne.

30 August. Bapaume and Noyon lost and evacuation of Flanders begins. Bailleul and Bullecourt-Hendecourt taken by the enemy but counterattack retakes the latter. Enemy penetrate Fresnes-Rouvroy line to take Hendecourt. On the Aisne, Juvigny lost to an American attack.

31 August. Péronne captured, Mount Kemmel evacuated and three tank attack against British positions near Cambrai repulsed. Heavy fighting on Mont St. Quentin with *2 Guard Division* losing 700 POWs during the Australian attack. Overall losses since the start of the enemy offensive amount to 228,000 with only 130,000 replacements available; ten divisions disbanded to stiffen remainder.

1 September. Enemy attacks on the Somme eliminate Amiens salient. North of Soissons five villages lost to French attacks and in Flanders Neuve Église and Wulverghem recaptured by the enemy.

2 September. Drocourt-Quéant switch line broken by enemy attack with the loss of 10,000 POWs; Ludendorff issues order for a second phased retirement to the main defences behind and along the Canal du Nord.

3 September. Rapid retirement around Lens and enemy re-enter the town; 6000 POWs lost. At Epenancourt, south of Péronne, French troops cross the river.

4 September. Ploegsteert and Hill 63 in Flanders, and Ruyaulcourt on the Somme, captured by the enemy.

5 September. French attack on the Somme pushes troops back across the Crozat Canal and captures Ham and five other villages. On the Aisne the Franco-American attack is held up at Allemant.

6 September. Lys salient completely evacuated and decision taken to halt retirement on the Hermann-Hunding-Brunhild position.

7 September. Minor fighting in Flanders and, on the Somme, Roisel rail junction lost.

8 September. Ludendorff orders St. Mihiel salient evacuation.

9 September. Counterattacks at Laffaux on the Aisne fail. To the north on the Somme, the enemy captures the high ground at Havrincourt Wood, overlooking the Siegfried Stellung.

11 September. Counterattacks at Gouzeaucourt and Moeuvres near Cambrai.

A captured British tank being used to tether horses.

Heavy artillery moving through Lens.

12 September. Troops endure a four-hour barrage, including 200 tons of Phosgene, before Franco-American attack on a twelve-mile front at St. Mihiel. Siegfried Stellung attacked near Cambrai on a three mile front; a four-division counterattack beaten off and 1000 POWs lost.

13 September. St. Mihiel salient closed by American troops who take 13,000 POWs.

14 September. Five counterattacks against advancing French forces at Allemant are repulsed with the loss of 2500 POWs.

15 September. Construction of Hermann line begun.

16 September. Four reserve divisions committed to the fighting at St. Mihiel but the salient is lost.

17 September. Further counterattacks near Cambrai fail, and, in Flanders, Canteleux trench is lost.

18 September. Enemy assault, on a sixteen-mile front, northwest of St. Quentin, results in the loss of Epéhy and 9000 POWs.

19 September. In fighting around Cambrai, Lempire and Essigny-Le-Grand are taken by the enemy.

21 September. Le Petit Priel Farm near Cambrai captured by the British.

22 September. Marwitz, commander of *Second Army*, is replaced by Carlowitz in order to take over command of Fifth Army from Gallwitz.

23 September. French troops push through positions and reach the River Oise north of La Fère.

24 September. High Command informs the government that armistice talks are inevitable. Over 30,000 men lost as POWs in the last week to the British alone. Further attacks on the Somme push troops back to within two miles of St. Quentin.

25 September. Counterattacks near Epéhy and Moeuvres against British positions fail.

26 September. Thirty-seven division Franco-American attack on a forty-mile front after three-hour bombardment against positions in the Meuse and Argonne; enemy break through and advance on average three miles.

27 September. Strengthening resistance slows down the enemy advance but Montfaucon and Varennes lost along with 23,000 POWs. At Cambrai British attack on a fourteen mile front and advance about three miles taking Bourlon Wood and Graincourt as well as 10,000 POWs and 200 guns. Some success at holding Seigfried Stellung outposts against American forces.

28 September. In Flanders the enemy attack on a twenty-three mile front after a three-hour barrage taking Houthulst Forest and Wytschaete along with 4,000 POWs. On the Aisne Front Italian troops cross east of Condé. Hindenburg and Ludendorff agree that Germany must request an immediate armistice.

29 September. Kaiser approves Hindenburg and Ludendorff's request for an armistice. Anglo-French units attack the Seigfried Stellung after a bombardment of nearly one million rounds. Enemy cross the St. Quentin Canal using boats, ladders and lifebelts, advancing 3½ miles and taking 4,200 POWs. In Flanders Dixmunde recaptured by Belgian troops, but further attacks by Belgian forces on Westroosebeke repelled.

30 September. Retiring troops set fire to buildings in Cambrai; enemy capture six villages on the outskirts of the town. In Champagne French forces take Marfaux-Aure and St. Marie-a-Py. In the Argonne, troops have retired eight miles and lost 18,000 men as POWs. Only fifty-nine of the 197 divisions now classed as fit. Ten divisions disbanded to provide troops for other divisions. Medium batteries reduced from four to three guns due to a shortage of horses. Bulgaria signs an armistice to end hostilities.

1 October. In the Champagne, troops fall back on a fourteen-mile front when French Army attacks. Wotan line breached by British troops and work begun on next two defence lines. Lens and Armentières evacuated during the night. Ludendorff sends a cable to Berlin government to transmit a peace offer without further delay.

2 October. Enemy held at Menin and Roulers junction. French enter a ruined St. Quentin.

3 October. British troops with tanks attack the Beaurevoir Line on an eight-mile front, capturing Le Catelet. In the Argonne American forces are held by the troops in the Apremont-Brieulles line. In Champagne the French take Challerange and the Americans storm Blanc Mont Ridge.

4 October. Enemy troops take Hill 240 and four villages west of the River Meuse; troops fall back on the Kriemhilde positions.

5 October. British capture Beaurevoir and troops withdraw from the Scheldt Canal. The order of the day from the Kaiser mentions a peace offer but urges the army to continue to offer stern resistance. Prior to withdrawing, Doaui is burned to make it useless to the enemy. In the Champagne troops withdraw along the entire front under pressure from the French and occupy Moronvillers Massif.

6 October. Laon set on fire before enemy arrive.

7 October. Berry-au-Bac on the Aisne captured by the French.

8 October. Enemy attack on a twenty-mile front between St. Quentin and Cambrai, taking the Fresnoy-Rouvroy line, Forenville, Niergnies and Villers-Outreaux along with 10,000 POWs; three local counter-attacks using four ATV tanks and captured British ones fail to recapture lost villages near Cambrai. Army Groups Boehn and Rupprecht ordered back to Hermann position – Boehn group to be split up and used by other armies.

9 October. Canadians enter Cambrai and British drive towards the River Selle.

10 October. British troops push on towards the Hermann position, along the Sensée Canal and retake Le Cateau.

11 October. Pressure on the flanks causes a general retirement between the rivers Meuse and Oise to the Hunding-Brunhild line. Army and Marine units hasten the speed of the evacuation of coastal bases and defences in Flanders. In Flanders Canadian troops capture Iwuy.

12 October. Retirement of *Sixth Army* sanctioned; Eberhardt replaces Mudra who replaces Below as commander of *Seventeenth Army* as the latter is recalled to Germany to organise home defence. British advance into Douai checked by deliberate flooding of the area. Hindenburg warns the troops that continued resistance is necessary to obtain favourable armistice terms.

13 October. La Fère and Laon fall to French troops.

14 October. Enemy renews offensive in Flanders with an attack between Dixmunde and the River Lys. Kriemhilde line attacked by American forces.

15 October. Belgian and British troops reach the River Lys.

16 October. Dunkirk shelled. Kriemhilde line breached by American troops and the French cross the river Aisne taking Vouziers Heights and Grandpré. *Sixth* and *Seventeenth* Armies ordered to retreat into the Hermann Line.

17 October. Lille evacuated and Ostend occupied by Belgian troops. American assault on Hermann positions takes 5000 POWs. Ludendorff demands a fight to the finish and states that an enemy breakthrough is unlikely.

18 October. Hunding line breached by French troops at the River Serre north of Laon.

19 October. In Flanders, Bruges and Zeebrugge are occupied by Belgian troops, while, in Artois, troops are pushed back nearly seven miles in a day and Denain is lost to advancing Canadians. On the River Lys the enemy takes Courtrai during a six-mile advance.

20 October. On the River Selle British troops storm the Hermann line and take Solesmes.

22 October. A four-mile Allied advance on the River Scheldt pushes troops out of the Fôret de Raismes and brings them close to Valenciennes.

23 October. Enemy open up the Selle defences on a thirty-five mile front, penetrating six miles deep.

24 October. Ludendorff asks men for continued resistance.

25 October. French attack on the Oise breaches the Hunding line, taking 150 POWs, and holds against counterattack. Final British thrust on the Selle pushes troops back to Le Quesnoy, Valenciennes and the edge of Mormal Forest.

26 October. Ludendorff resigns and is succeeded by Gröner. The Kaiser refuses Hindenburg's resignation.

27 October. Attack northwest of Le Quesnoy repulsed by British troops. Troops defending Grandpré retire after holding the Americans at bay for two days.

28 October. Counterattack on Mont Houy pushes British back.

29 October. Guise in the Oise region falls to French pressure.

30 October. *18 Landwehr Division* refuses to go back in to the front line. Turkey signs an armistice with

A destroyed British artillery position.

hostilities to cease from 31 October.

31 October. The Kaiser travels to Army HQ in Spa. Troops pushed back to the River Scheldt by British advance.

1 November. Counterattack using captured tanks fails to push Canadian troops of Mont Houy. British attacks push troops back towards Maubege, Mons and the River Dendre. American attack drives a five-mile wedge into positions at Bourgogne, overrunning four divisions after a 36,000 round barrage of Mustard gas.

2 November. Reinforcements from the Eastern Front mutiny on the Sambre Front and have to be disarmed. Valenciennes is taken by Canadian troops who capture 1800 POWs. Buzancy falls after American attack.

3 November. Austro-Hungarians sign an armistice with hostilities to end on 4 November.

4 November. Enemy attack on a thirty-mile front between Valenciennes pushes defending troops back five miles, taking 10,000 POWs.

5 November. General withdrawal of troops on the Sambre to the Antwerp-Meuse position ordered and the general withdrawal of men from the Meuse to Condé on the Scheldt begins.

6 November. Stout defence by *Seventeenth Army* rearguards slows down British advance on the Sambre but Army Group Gallwitz is ordered to fall back to the Antwerp-Meuse position. Over 1700 POWs lost during Canadian attack north of Valenciennes.

7 November. Troops pushed back by British attack west of Maubege.

8 November. Armistice delegates meet with Foch. Troops withdraw in the Scheldt sector and retire from the Hermann position near Tournai.

9 November. The Kaiser abdicates. General retreat on the Scheldt front and Maubege falls to the enemy in the Sambre sector. On the Aisne French troops capture Hirson rail junction.

10 November. Stiff resistance by machine gun troops slows down enemy advance in to Mons, but town falls by dawn.

11 November. Armistice signed and hostilities cease at 11am.

13 November. Troops begin general retirement to Germany.

14 November. Munitions dump south of Namur blown up by retiring troops.

18 November. As the last troops leave French territory, a munitions dump east of Namur is blown up.

22 November. Last troops leave Luxembourg.

26 November. Final troops in Belgium cross into Germany.

With ever increasing demands for men the age of garrison troops rose.

A trench mortar in position before the offensive.

Clearing the dead from the battlefield.

A supply column at rest. The ever increasing distances between the front positions and the ability of the supply wagons to keep up meant that many soldiers went hungry for days.

A captured French Schneider tank being taken away for inspection.

Field artillery in place for attacks in the French sector of the front.

Wood was an essential part of the war effort being used by the ton in the construction of trenches.

Light artillery temporarily dug in before following the advance.

Kemmel after the fighting had moved on.

Infantry following the artillery barrage.

Older soldiers, playing cards behind the lines. On the wall is a poster describing the prizes taken by the German Army in the first month of the offensive: 127,000 POWs, 1,600 guns, around 1,000 machine guns and about 200 tanks.

How different was life on the Eastern Front!

A captured British tank being used by German forces.

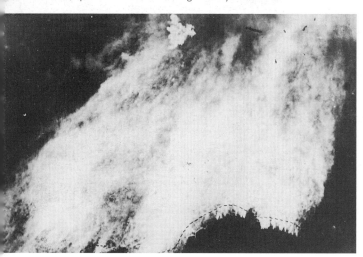

Aerial view of a gas attack.

A new cemetery to accommodate the dead from the June 1918 battles.

A defensive position in the new line to hold off the Allied forces.

Wounded troops waiting to be taken to hospital left by the roadside to be collected by ambulance.

American troops learning to deal with the mud that appeared rapidly after a downpour.

With fires raging in the distance, German troops rest in a field.

Gefreiter Johann Seigl of *1 Bavarian Infantry Regiment*, killed in action on 21 August 1918.

August 1918 – the war was approaching its end but the regimental sports continued. Here *65 Infantry Regiment* gather to putt the shot.

Zum
frommen
Andenken
im Gebete

an den
jugend-
samen
Jüngling

Johann Geigl

Kölblbauernsohn von Leobendorf,

Gefrt. beim 1. bayr. Inf.-Regt., 3. Komp.,
Inhaber des Eisernen Kreuzes und des
Verdienstkreuzes mit Schwertern,

welcher nach 42 monatlicher, treuer Pflicht-
erfüllung am 21. August 1918 durch Brust-
schuß, im Alter von 23 Jahren den
Heldentod fürs Vaterland starb.

Er starb den Tod auf heißerkämpften Auen,
Fürs hart bedrängte Vaterland.
Nie werden wir ihm mehr ins Auge schauen
Und ihm nicht drücken mehr die Hand.
Er wird uns fehlen wenn die Brüder wiederkehren,
Nach hartem Kampf — zurück ins Vaterhaus.
Und unser Schmerz wird doppelt sich vermehren,
Vergeblich schaut das Auge nach ihm aus. —

O Herr gib ihm und allen gefallenen
Kriegern die ewige Ruhe!

Druck von Fritz Keerl, Laufen.

With the Allied forces gaining the upper hand, the German army started an orderly retreat whenever possible. *160 Infantry Regiment* is seen here leaving Gouzeaucourt.

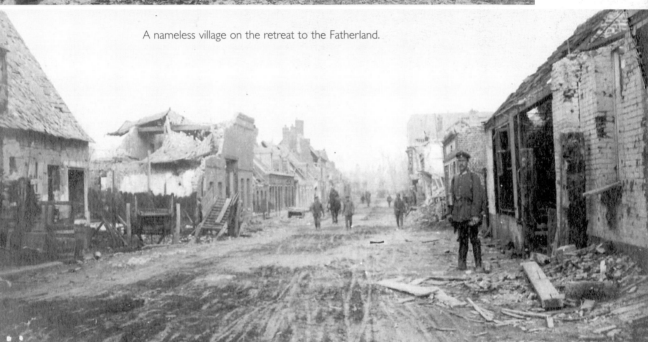

A nameless village on the retreat to the Fatherland.

French dead in the Argonne region during the German retreat.

St. Mihiel before the Americans arrived.

An abandoned field gun during the retreat.

Belleau Wood – American troops advance ignoring the dead and wounded Germans on the road.

American advance, wounded and dying Germans spread along the road. Belleau Wood – France

German prisoners being transported to a POW camp by their American captors.

A photo for the folks at home: American troops in a ruined house in St. Mihiel after the battle.

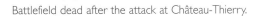
Battlefield dead after the attack at Château-Thierry.

German troops begin the long march home.

A retreating army comes home as heroes.

The long and lonely march continues.

Just before Christmas Bavarian troops arrive home to a heroes welcome.

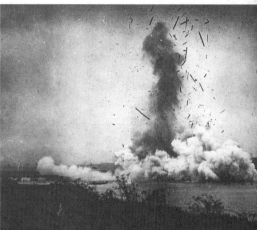

The last shot of the war on the American front destroyed a bridge.

Troops arriving home to a hereos' welcome as guardians of the free Republic.

Troops captured near the end of the war land in Britain to begin their captivity.

Kapitän König mit seinen Offizieren und der Mannschaft an Bord des Frachttauchbootes „Deutschland" nach dem Eintreffen auf der Wesermündung

Ocean Comfort Co. m. b. H., Bremerhaven

While the major battle front had been the Western Front, German success had relied heavily on the U-boat offensive – this photo shows the crew of Kapitän Königs' U-boat 'Deutschland', a blockade runner submarine that became U-155 when America entered the war.

Four years putting up barbed wire. Taking it down would keep POWs occupied for some considerable time after the war.

After the troops withdrew, the only Germans on the Western Front were the POWs or the dead.

With the war over many soldiers returned home, but some stayed on to work for the Armistice Commission.

The soldier of 1918, in many cases, became the Freikorps soldier of 1919.

A British base over-run during the March offensive.

Bibliography

Becke, Major A.F. *Military Operations France & Belgium, 1918* volume 1. Macmillan & Co, 1935

Chickering, R. *Imperial Germany and the Great War, 1914-1918.* Cambridge University Press, 2005

Edmonds, Brigadier General Sir James, CB, CMG. *Military operations 1917, Volume 2, Messines and 3rd Ypres.* HMSO, 1948

Edmonds, Brigadier General Sir James, CB, CMG. *Military operations France & Belgium 1918,* volume 2. Macmillan & Co, 1937

Edmonds, Brigadier General Sir James, CB, CMG. *Military operations France & Belgium 1918,* volume 3. Macmillan & Co, 1939

Edmonds, Brigadier General Sir James, CB, CMG. *Military operations France & Belgium 1918,* volume 4. HMSO, 1947

Edmonds, Brigadier General Sir James, CB, CMG. *Military operations France & Belgium 1918,* volume 5. HMSO, 1947

Falls, Captain C. *Military operations France & Belgium 1917. The German retreat to the Hindenburg line and the battle of Arras.* Macmillan, 1940

Gray, R & Argyle, C. *Chronicle of the First World War Volume 1, 1914-1916.* Facts on File, 1991

Gray, R & Argyle, C. *Chronicle of the First World War Volume 2, 1917-1921.* Facts on File, 1991

Hull, I. *Absolute destruction.* Cornell University Press, 2005

Keegan, J. *Passchendaele, Volume 6 History of the First World War.* Purnell, 1971

Kitchen, M. *The German offensives of 1918.* Tempus, 2005

Ludendorff, General. *My war memories 1914-1918* volume 2. Hutchinson (No Date)

Middlebrook, M. *The Kaiser's Battle.* Allen Lane, 1978

Miles, Captain W. *Military operations France & Belgium 1917. The battle of Cambrai.* HMSO, 1949

Passingham, I. *All the Kaiser's men.* Sutton Publishing, 2003

Sheldon, J. *The German Army on the Somme 1914-1916.* Pen & Sword, 2005

Thomas, N. *The German Army in World War 1 (3) 1917-18.* Osprey, 2004

Williams, J. *The Home Fronts 1914-1918.* Constable, 1972